QUICK FROM SCRATCH

PASTA

Cavatappi with Pepperoni, page 137

QUICK FROM SCRATCH
PASTA

Food & Wine
BOOKS

American Express Publishing Corporation
New York

Editor in Chief: Judith Hill
Assistant Editors: Susan Lantzius and Laura Byrne Russell
Managing Editor: Terri Mauro
Copy Editor: Barbara A. Mateer
Wine Editor: Richard Marmet
Contributing Editor: Judith Sutton
Art Director: Nina Scerbo
Photographer: Melanie Acevedo
Photo Editor: Shelley Thomas
Food Stylist: Roscoe Betsill
Prop Stylist: Denise Canter
Portrait Photographer: Christopher Dinerman
Production Manager: Stuart Handelman

Senior Vice President/Chief Marketing Officer: Mark V. Stanich
Vice President, Books and Products: Marshall A. Corey
Marketing Manager: Bruce Spanier
Senior Fulfillment Manager: Phil Black
Business Manager: Doreen Camardi
Marketing Coordinator: Richard Nogueira

Cover Design: Perri DeFino
Recipe Pictured on Front Cover: Fettuccine with Veal, Peas, and Mint, page 169

AMERICAN EXPRESS PUBLISHING CORPORATION

LIBRARY OF CONGRESS CATALOGING-IN-PUBLICATION DATA AVAILABLE

ISBN 0-916103-87-0

Published by American Express Publishing Corporation
1120 Avenue of the Americas, New York, NY 10036

Printed in China.

CONTENTS

RECIPES PICTURED ABOVE: (*left to right*) pages 59, 109, 161

Taste-testing a new pasta during development of this book

Susan Lantzius trained at La Varenne École de Cuisine in Paris, worked as a chef in Portugal for a year, and then headed to New York City. There she made her mark first as head decorator at the well-known Sant Ambroeus pastry shop and next as a pastry chef, working at such top restaurants as San Domenico and Maxim's. In 1993, she turned her talents to recipe development and editorial work for FOOD & WINE Books.

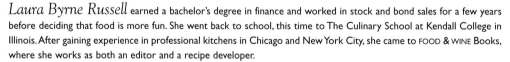

Judith Hill is the editor in chief of FOOD & WINE Books, a division of American Express Publishing. Previously she was editor in chief of COOK'S Magazine, director of publications for La Varenne École de Cuisine in Paris, from which she earned a Grand Diplôme, and an English instructor for the University of Maryland International Division in Germany. Her book credits include editing cookbooks for Fredy Girardet, Jane Grigson, Michel Guérard, and Anne Willan.

Laura Byrne Russell earned a bachelor's degree in finance and worked in stock and bond sales for a few years before deciding that food is more fun. She went back to school, this time to The Culinary School at Kendall College in Illinois. After gaining experience in professional kitchens in Chicago and New York City, she came to FOOD & WINE Books, where she works as both an editor and a recipe developer.

INTRODUCTION

I feel relatively safe saying that pasta lends itself to more quick and varied preparations than any other food on earth. Who doesn't eat pasta at least once during the rush of the working week? And there's some delectable pasta dish for everyone, from the vegetarian to Jack Sprat's wife.

In writing this book, our star recipe developers, Susan Lantzius and Laura Russell, came up with the full range of familiar combinations such as peppers and sausage, Parmesan and cream, clams and tomato sauce—and also with some wild thoughts. Brussels sprouts, Laura said out of the blue one day. I have to admit, I had no enthusiasm for the thought of sprouts and pasta—in fact, very little interest in Brussels sprouts at all. But I love the Pasta Shells with Chicken and Brussels Sprouts, page 105, that she developed; the mild chicken balances the sprouts perfectly. When Laura suggested melted cream cheese as the base for a sauce, I was skeptical. Yet even though it's hard to choose pets from this collection of recipes, the Spaghetti with Creamy Spinach and Tarragon, page 39, is one of my favorites; and guess what the creaminess comes from. Oranges with pasta? Yup. Susan's Bow-Tie Salad with Scallops, Black Olives, Oranges, and Mint, page 85, is truly delectable and makes an ideal, refreshing summer supper.

We've used pepperoni, peanut butter, salami, sweet potatoes, melon, avocado, and dried apricots. Any ingredient that you can get easily in the supermarket was fair game. Not that strange novelty was the aim. Speed and deliciousness were the goals—goals that are met in every single recipe that made it into this book.

We hope you'll find many dishes here, whether based on tradition or invention, that give you both welcome speed in the kitchen and supreme satisfaction at the table. And also that you'll feel free to experiment with our variations on the recipes and with your own ideas. Think of the recipes as outlines and fill them in with what you have on hand. Take our word for it, though—pasta and bananas just don't work together.

Judith Hill
Editor in Chief
FOOD & WINE Books

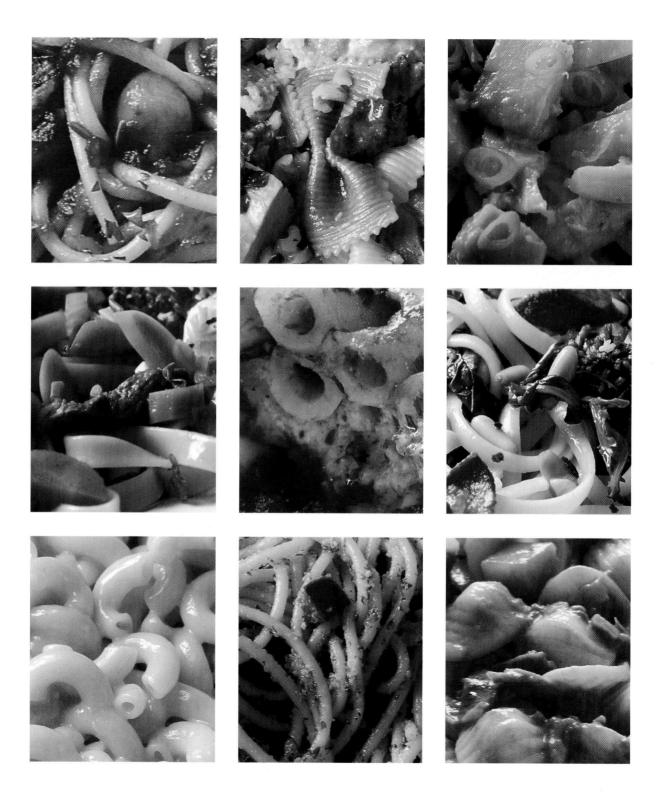

Before You Begin

You'll find test-kitchen tips and ideas for ingredient substitutions presented with the individual recipes throughout this book. In this opening section, we've gathered information and tips that apply to all, or at least a substantial number, of the recipes. These are the facts and opinions that we'd like you to know before you use, and to keep in mind while you use, the recipes. We hope you'll read these pages prior to cooking from the book for the first time—and have kept the section short so that you can do so with ease. The culinary information here will help make your cooking quicker, simpler, and even tastier.

RECIPES PICTURED OPPOSITE: (top) pages 95, 97, 81; (center) pages 121, 65, 147; (bottom) pages 61, 69, 145

Pasta Wheel
SUBSTITUTING PASTA SHAPES

For each recipe, we chose the pasta carefully to match its shape to the sauce. However, this doesn't mean that you have to keep two dozen varieties of pasta on hand at all times. Most recipes are just as good when you substitute another kind. Use the wheel below to help you choose the best alternative.

How to use the pasta wheel

Around the edge of the wheel are the various pastas we call for in this book. In the center are five basic types that many people have in the cupboard. To use the wheel, find the pasta on the outer circle that you would like to replace. Look toward the middle for the basic variety that you can use as a substitute. For instance, if the recipe specifies fusilli, use shells instead. Of course, you can also interchange any pasta within a section. In that fusilli recipe, you could just as well go with rotelle.

Your own basic five might be different from the ones shown here. If you love bow ties, stock them instead of shells. And if you want to keep only four shapes, use spaghetti in place of spaghettini and the other long, thin shapes in that section.

All the pastas grouped with fettuccine contain eggs. We include stuffed shapes, like tortellini and ravioli, in this section since they are always made with egg pasta. You'll find that plain and stuffed egg pastas are surprisingly interchangeable in most recipes, though of course the final effect will differ somewhat depending upon your choice. Note that fettuccine is also sold in an eggless version. Look at the package; if the pasta contains eggs this will be clearly stated. Ideally, you'll use an egg pasta in the recipes that specify fettuccine, egg noodles, or stuffed pasta, but you can still use eggless fettuccine with good results.

How Do You Know When the Pasta's Done?

There are two good ways to tell when pasta is done: break it and look at it, or bite into it. When you break a cooked piece of pasta in half, there should be no opaque white core. Test periodically; as soon as that core has disappeared, the pasta is ready. Alternatively, when you bite it, it should feel cooked through but still resilient, not flabby.

This list is for your easy reference when substituting one pasta type for another. Though the cooking times look precise, don't let them fool you. They may vary depending on the brand of pasta you use, the amount of water, and your altitude. These are the times that worked for us in the test kitchen, and they'll certainly get you close to the mark.

PASTA SHAPE	COOKING TIME (minutes)	PASTA SHAPE	COOKING TIME (minutes)
Bow Ties	15	Perciatelli	15
Cavatappi	13	Rigatoni	14
Egg Noodles (wide)	3	Rotelle	12
Elbow Macaroni	8	Shells (medium)	10
Fedelini	6	Spaghetti	12
Fettuccine	12	Spaghettini	9
Fusilli	13	Tortellini (fresh)	4
Linguine	12	Tortellini (frozen)	12
Linguine Piccole	9	Vermicelli	9
Orecchiette	15	Whole-Wheat Linguine	12
Penne	13	Whole-Wheat Spaghetti	15
Penne Rigate	13	Ziti	13

ESSENTIAL INGREDIENT INFORMATION

Broth, Chicken

We tested all of the recipes in this book using canned low-sodium chicken broth. You can substitute regular for low-sodium broth; just cut back on the salt in the recipe. And if you keep homemade stock in your freezer, by all means feel free to use it. We aren't suggesting that it won't work as well, only that we know the dishes taste delicious even when made with canned broth.

Butter

Our recipes don't specify whether to use salted or unsalted butter. We generally use unsalted, but in these savory dishes, it really won't make a big difference which type you use.

Cheese, Grated

We frequently call for Parmesan cheese in our recipes. Not only is it widely available, but it's hard to beat real fresh-grated Parmigiano-Reggiano. However, Parmesan has become something of a generic term including all Italian grating cheeses and we use it in that sense. Feel free to substitute Romano or Asiago.

Chorizo

When we refer to chorizo sausage in our recipes, we mean the readily available cured pork sausage seasoned with paprika and usually garlic, commonly referred to as Spanish-style. Pepperoni or another spicy hard sausage makes a good substitute.

Coconut Milk

Coconut milk is the traditional liquid used in many Thai and Indian curries. Make sure you buy *unsweetened* canned coconut milk, not cream of coconut, which is used primarily for piña coladas. Heavy cream can be substituted in many recipes.

Garlic

■ The size of garlic cloves varies tremendously. When we call for one minced or chopped clove, we expect you to get about ¾ teaspoon.
■ By *smashed garlic*, we mean crushed, but not to a paste. Put the flat of the blade of a large knife over the clove and smack the blade a couple of times or just press down on it firmly.

Mustard

When we call for mustard, we mean Dijon or grainy. We never, ever mean yellow ballpark mustard.

Oil

Cooking oil in these recipes refers to readily available, reasonably priced nut, seed, or vegetable oil with a high smoking point, such as peanut, sunflower, canola, safflower, or corn oil. These can be heated to about 400° before they begin to smoke, break down, and develop an unpleasant flavor.

Olives

If your store doesn't sell olives from big, open barrels, opt for the kind in jars. The canned version gives you only the slightest hint of what a real olive might taste like.

Parsley

Many of our recipes call for chopped fresh parsley. The flat-leaf variety has a stronger flavor than the curly, and we use it most of the time, but unless the type is specified, you can use either.

Pepper

- There's nothing like fresh-ground pepper. If you've been using preground, buy a pepper mill, fill it, and give it a grind. You'll never look back.
- To measure your just-ground pepper more easily, become familiar with your own mill; each produces a different amount per turn. You'll probably find that 10 to 15 grinds produces ¼ teaspoon of pepper, and then you can count on that forever after.

Tomatoes, Canned

In some recipes, we call for "crushed tomatoes in thick puree." Depending on the brand, this mix of crushed tomatoes and tomato puree may be labeled crushed tomatoes with puree, with added puree, in tomato puree, thick style, or in thick puree. You can use any of these.

Wine, Dry White

Leftover wine is ideal for cooking. It seems a shame to open a fresh bottle for just a few spoonfuls. Another solution is to keep dry vermouth on hand. You can use whatever quantity is needed; the rest will keep indefinitely.

Zest

Citrus zest—the colored part of the peel, without any of the white pith—adds tremendous flavor to many a dish. Remove the zest from the fruit using either a grater or a zester. A zester is a small, inexpensive, and extremely handy tool. It has little holes that remove just the zest in fine ribbons. A zester is quick, easy to clean, and never scrapes your knuckles.

Faster, Better, Easier
TEST-KITCHEN TIPS

First, boil the water

The very first thing you should do when you walk into the kitchen is put a pot of water on the stove to boil. You can make most of the sauces in this book in the time it takes to boil water and cook the pasta. You don't want to get to the end of a recipe and realize you have to stand around and wait while the water heats up.

Salting water

For a ¾ pound batch of pasta, use about 3 quarts of water and 1½ tablespoons of salt. This may seem like a lot of salt, but it's just enough to give the water a slightly salty flavor. Taste the water; if it doesn't taste like anything, neither will your cooked pasta.

Scheduling the sauce

You can make the sauces in this book and let them sit for a few minutes while the pasta cooks. Tossing the sauce with the hot pasta will bring it right back to life. You can also, for even greater speed, make the sauce and cook the pasta simultaneously.

Tossing the pasta and sauce

When we say "toss the pasta with the sauce," you have three alternatives:

1. Drain the pasta, return it to the hot pot, and toss in the sauce and any additional ingredients. Most of the time, this is the quickest method. It also has the advantages of minimizing dirty dishes and keeping the pasta warmer than tossing it in a separate bowl.

2. If you've cooked the sauce in a large enough pan, you can do the reverse—drain the pasta and toss it directly into the pan of hot sauce.

3. Toss the pasta and sauce together in a large bowl. This method is good when you're using a soft cheese, such as fresh mozzarella, that may get stringy due to the heat from the pot. Also use this method when the recipe includes a large quantity of fresh basil. The heat can discolor the herb.

Thinning sauce

Before draining pasta, ladle out some of the water; it will come in handy if your sauce is too thick. Because pasta cooking water contains starch, it thins a sauce and adds a bit of body at the same time. Just stir in as much as needed.

Peeling garlic

To peel a garlic clove, use a large knife. Put the flat of the blade over the garlic and smack the blade with your fist or the heel of your hand. The clove will crack, and the skin will loosen and come off easily.

Break it up

Whole canned tomatoes can be chopped before adding them to the sauce or broken up in the pan with the side of a spoon. The easiest way, though, is to squeeze the tomatoes through your fingers into the pan. Messy, but quick.

The salad bar as prep chef

Most grocery stores have a salad bar stocked with fresh, precut ingredients that can save you time. Look for:

- broccoli florets
- cantaloupe wedges
- cut carrots
- cauliflower florets
- sliced celery
- grated cheese
- sliced cucumbers
- diced ham
- sliced mushrooms
- chopped red or white onions
- sliced green peppers
- pineapple chunks
- chopped scallions
- cleaned spinach
- tomato wedges

Not only will you save time, but when you need only a small quantity, you may even save money.

No substitutions here

Certain ingredients just cannot be dried, bottled, jarred, or powdered and still retain good flavor. We beg you to use only fresh:

- parsley
- basil
- cilantro
- onions
- garlic
- lemon juice

Regulating the heat of chile peppers

The heat of chile peppers, such as jalapeños, is concentrated in the ribs and seeds. If you prefer a milder chile flavor, remove these; if your taste is for hot, include them, or at least some of them. Since the heat level varies wildly from one chile to another, even within the same variety, you'll need to taste while you're cooking. If you remove the ribs and seeds, reserve them. Then if the dish could stand more heat, you can always add them to taste.

Vegetables & Cheese

PENNE WITH ROASTED ASPARAGUS AND BALSAMIC BUTTER

Simmering the balsamic vinegar both mellows and thickens it. When tossed with the hot pasta and the butter, it forms a smooth, uniquely flavored sauce.

WINE RECOMMENDATION

Balsamic vinegar, Parmesan cheese, and especially asparagus will be best served by a wine with plenty of acidity. Look for a Sancerre from the Loire Valley in France (made from sauvignon blanc grapes) or a sauvignon blanc from Italy.

SERVES 4

- 1 pound asparagus
- 1 tablespoon olive oil
- 2 teaspoons salt
- 1/2 teaspoon fresh-ground black pepper
- 1/2 cup plus 2 tablespoons balsamic vinegar
- 1/2 teaspoon brown sugar
- 1 pound penne
- 1/4 pound butter, cut into pieces
- 1/3 cup grated Parmesan cheese, plus more for serving

1. Heat the oven to 400°. Snap the tough ends off the asparagus and discard them. Cut the spears into 1-inch pieces. Put the asparagus on a baking sheet and toss with the oil and 1/4 teaspoon each of the salt and pepper. Roast until tender, about 10 minutes.

2. Meanwhile, put the vinegar in a small saucepan. Simmer until 3 tablespoons remain. Stir in the brown sugar and the remaining 1/4 teaspoon pepper. Remove from the heat.

3. Cook the penne in a large pot of boiling, salted water until just done, about 13 minutes. Drain the pasta and toss with the butter, vinegar, asparagus, Parmesan, and the remaining 1 3/4 teaspoons salt. Serve with additional Parmesan.

VARIATIONS

PENNE WITH ROASTED BROCCOLI AND BALSAMIC BUTTER

When asparagus is not in season, cut 1 pound of broccoli into small spears for roasting. Toss them with 2 tablespoons oil and 1/4 teaspoon each of salt and pepper and roast for about 15 minutes. Continue with step 2.

PENNE WITH ROASTED VEGETABLES, TOASTED NUTS, AND BALSAMIC BUTTER

Toss in 1/3 cup of toasted pine nuts, hazelnuts, or walnuts at the end with either asparagus or broccoli.

FETTUCCINE ALFREDO WITH ASPARAGUS

Ready to go at a moment's notice, this asparagus-embellished classic is not only creamy, quick, and delicious, but it dirties only one pot.

WINE RECOMMENDATION
A forcefully acidic white wine is a natural with asparagus and will pierce the richness of the sauce. Try one of the sauvignon blancs from New Zealand or a vernaccia from Italy.

SERVES 4

- 1 pound asparagus
- ¾ pound fettuccine
- 4 tablespoons butter, cut into pieces
- 1 cup heavy cream
  Pinch grated nutmeg
- ¾ teaspoon salt
- ⅛ teaspoon fresh-ground black pepper
- ½ cup grated Parmesan cheese, plus more for serving

1. Snap the tough ends off the asparagus and discard them. Cut the asparagus spears into 1-inch pieces. In a large pot of boiling, salted water, cook the fettuccine until almost done, about 8 minutes. Add the asparagus; cook until it and the pasta are just done, about 4 minutes longer.

2. Drain the pasta and asparagus. Toss with the butter, cream, nutmeg, salt, pepper, and Parmesan. Serve with additional Parmesan.

VARIATIONS

FETTUCCINE ALFREDO
Eliminate the asparagus.

FETTUCCINE ALFREDO WITH HAM AND PEAS
Eliminate the asparagus. Add 1 cup frozen peas to the pasta during the last 2 minutes of cooking. Toss ¼ pound of deli ham, cut into matchstick strips, with the remaining ingredients.

FETTUCCINE ALFREDO WITH FRESH MIXED HERBS
Eliminate the asparagus. Toss in 3 tablespoons of chopped fresh herbs, such as basil, parsley, and/or chives, at the end.

FETTUCCINE ALFREDO WITH PARSLEY AND SAGE
Eliminate the asparagus. Toss in 2 tablespoons chopped fresh parsley and ½ teaspoon dried sage at the end.

Pasta Shells with Portobello Mushrooms, Asparagus, and Boursin Sauce

Boursin, a French cheese available in most supermarkets, melts smoothly to make an appetizing sauce. We call for pepper Boursin, but the dish is equally good with the herb-and-garlic version; just add a little fresh-ground black pepper to the finished pasta.

WINE RECOMMENDATION
Asparagus is best with a high-acid white wine such as a Bordeaux blanc from France or a California sauvignon blanc. These wines will also balance the rich cheese.

SERVES 4

- 1 tablespoon butter
- 1 tablespoon olive oil
- 1 pound portobello mushrooms, stems removed, caps halved and then cut crosswise into 1/4-inch slices
- 1/2 teaspoon salt
- 1 1/4 cups canned low-sodium chicken broth or homemade stock
- 1 5 1/2-ounce package pepper Boursin cheese
- 1 pound asparagus
- 3/4 pound medium pasta shells

1. In a large frying pan, melt the butter with the oil over moderate heat. Add the mushrooms and salt and cook, stirring occasionally, until the mushrooms are tender and well browned, about 8 minutes. Add the chicken broth and Boursin cheese and bring to a simmer while stirring.

2. Snap the tough ends off the asparagus and discard them. Cut the spears into 1/2-inch pieces. In a large pot of boiling, salted water, cook the pasta until almost done, about 6 minutes. Add the asparagus and cook until it and the pasta are just done, about 4 minutes longer. Drain. Toss with the mushrooms and sauce.

Convenient Portobellos

Many stores carry packages of already stemmed and sliced portobello mushrooms, a real convenience. You can use ten ounces of the presliced portobello caps in place of the one pound of whole mushrooms we call for here.

FUSILLI WITH ARTICHOKE HEARTS AND PARMESAN CREAM

The spiral shape of the fusilli scoops up plenty of creamy sauce. This pasta would also make a nice side dish with roasted meat or chicken, in which case it would serve six.

WINE RECOMMENDATION

Artichokes usually make wines seem sweeter. Accordingly, we suggest a red or white wine with loads of acidity. A barbera or dolcetto from the Piedmont region of Italy or an Italian pinot bianco or sauvignon blanc would all be suitable.

SERVES 4

- 2 tablespoons butter
- 2 cloves garlic, minced
- 1 cup heavy cream
- ¾ teaspoon salt
- 1 teaspoon fresh-ground black pepper
- 2½ cups canned, drained artichoke hearts (two 14-ounce cans), rinsed and cut into halves or quarters
- ¾ pound fusilli
- ½ cup grated Parmesan cheese
- 2 tablespoons chopped chives, scallion tops, or parsley

1. In a medium saucepan, melt the butter over moderately low heat. Add the garlic and cook for 30 seconds. Stir in the cream, salt, pepper, and artichoke hearts. Cook until just heated through, about 3 minutes.

2. In a large pot of boiling, salted water, cook the fusilli until just done, about 13 minutes. Drain the pasta and toss with the cream sauce, Parmesan, and chives.

CANNED VS. MARINATED ARTICHOKE HEARTS

We vastly prefer canned artichoke hearts to the marinated type that come in small jars. The marinated ones often have an acrid taste. When using the canned artichokes, drain and rinse them first to remove any "tinny" flavor from the can.

ORECCHIETTE WITH BROCCOLI, ROASTED GARLIC, AND PINE NUTS

Robust roasted garlic pairs with the broccoli and chewy orecchiette perfectly. And a good sprinkling of Parmesan cheese adds the finishing touch. This pasta also tastes great with a bit of spiciness; if you like, add a pinch of red-pepper flakes to the garlic oil as soon as you remove it from the oven.

WINE RECOMMENDATION
Look for a crisp and zippy white wine such as a sauvignon blanc from the northern part of Italy. It will hold its own with the cheese, oil, and nuts and also complement the broccoli.

SERVES 4

1	head garlic, separated into cloves
1/3	cup olive oil
1/4	cup pine nuts
1/2	teaspoon salt
1/4	teaspoon fresh-ground black pepper
1 1/2	pounds broccoli, cut into small florets
3/4	pound orecchiette
1/4	cup grated Parmesan cheese, plus more for serving

1. Heat the oven to 325°. In a small oven-proof dish, toss the garlic with the oil. Cover with foil and roast until soft, about 30 minutes. Put the pine nuts in a separate pan and toast alongside the garlic until golden brown, about 15 minutes.

2. When the garlic is cool enough to handle, squeeze the flesh out of the peelings and mash the garlic into the warm oil remaining in the baking dish. Add the salt and pepper.

3. In a medium saucepan, steam or boil the broccoli until just done. Steaming will take about 5 minutes and boiling will take about 2.

4. In a large pot of boiling, salted water, cook the orecchiette until just done, about 15 minutes. Reserve 1/2 cup of the pasta water. Drain the orecchiette and toss with 1/4 cup of the reserved pasta water, the broccoli, the garlic mixture, the pine nuts, and the Parmesan. If the pasta seems dry, add more of the reserved pasta water. Serve with additional Parmesan.

SAVE THE STEMS

Though we use only the florets from the broccoli in this pasta, don't throw away the unused stems. Peel and slice them and add to a stir-fry or vegetable soup or use as a vegetable in their own right, either sautéed in olive oil with a little garlic or boiled and buttered.

LINGUINE WITH CAULIFLOWER, PINE NUTS, AND CURRANTS

With its brown-butter sauce, garlic, and Parmesan cheese, this pasta recipe combines flavors from both Northern and Southern Italy.

WINE RECOMMENDATION
The nuts and fruit, together with the assertive flavor of the cauliflower, are best with an acidic white wine. A bottle of Arneis or vernaccia from Italy, or alternatively a reasonably priced sparkling wine from California, would be a good choice.

SERVES 4

⅓	cup pine nuts
1	medium head cauliflower (about 2½ pounds), cut into small florets
½	cup currants or raisins
½	cup water
¾	teaspoon salt
6	tablespoons butter
2	tablespoons olive oil
4	cloves garlic, minced
¼	teaspoon dried red-pepper flakes
¾	pound linguine
¼	cup grated Parmesan cheese, plus more for serving
3	tablespoons chopped flat-leaf parsley

1. Heat the oven to 350°. Toast the pine nuts until golden brown, about 8 minutes.

2. Put the cauliflower in a large frying pan. Add the currants, water, and ¼ teaspoon of the salt. Bring to a simmer over moderate heat and cook, covered, until the cauliflower is almost tender, about 3 minutes. Remove the mixture from the pan.

3. Put the butter in the pan and cook over moderate heat, stirring, until the butter is golden brown, about 3 minutes. Add the cauliflower mixture, the oil, garlic, red-pepper flakes, and the remaining ½ teaspoon salt and cook, stirring, for 1 minute.

4. In a large pot of boiling, salted water, cook the linguine until just done, about 12 minutes. Reserve ¾ cup of the pasta water. Drain the linguine and toss with ½ cup of the reserved pasta water, the cauliflower mixture, pine nuts, Parmesan, and parsley. If the pasta seems dry, add more of the reserved pasta water. Serve with additional Parmesan.

Orecchiette with Indian-Spiced Cauliflower and Peas

Vegetables play an important role in the cuisine of India, and cauliflower and peas are a favorite combination. Here Italian orecchiette catches the peas and the sauce so that each bite is full of flavor.

WINE RECOMMENDATION
Fragrant sauces work very nicely with fragrant wines such as gewürztraminers, which can come from either the Alsace region in France or from California. The Alsatian version often has more acidity.

SERVES 4

2 tablespoons cooking oil

1 onion, cut into thin slices

2 cloves garlic, chopped

1¼ teaspoons ground cumin

1¼ teaspoons ground coriander

½ head cauliflower, cut into small florets (about 4 cups)

½ cup water

1½ cups canned crushed tomatoes (one 16-ounce can)

1 teaspoon salt

1 cup frozen petit peas

⅓ cup chopped cilantro

¾ pound orecchiette

1. In a large frying pan, heat the oil over moderately low heat. Add the onion and cook until starting to soften, about 3 minutes. Stir in the garlic, cumin, and coriander and cook until fragrant, 2 minutes longer.

2. Add the cauliflower to the onion mixture; stir to coat. Add the water, bring to a simmer, cover, and steam for 3 minutes. Stir in the tomatoes and salt. Reduce the heat and simmer, covered, for 10 minutes. Add the peas and cilantro and cook until the cauliflower is tender and the peas are hot, about 2 minutes longer.

3. In a large pot of boiling, salted water, cook the orecchiette until just done, about 15 minutes. Drain and toss with the sauce.

SPAGHETTINI WITH MUSHROOMS, GARLIC, AND OIL

We've added sautéed mushrooms to the classic—and very simple—spaghetti with garlic and oil, but the dish can still be made in no time at all. Regular white mushrooms are excellent here; portobellos or wild mushrooms would be great, too.

WINE RECOMMENDATION

The earthy taste of mushrooms goes wonderfully with the correspondingly earthy flavor of a pinot noir, while the assertive flavor of the garlic calls for a simple version of this wine. A bottle of Givry, Rully, or Mercurey from France will be your best choice.

SERVES 4

½ cup olive oil

3 cloves garlic, minced

⅛ teaspoon dried red-pepper flakes (optional)

⅔ pound mushrooms, sliced

1 teaspoon salt

1 pound spaghettini

3 tablespoons chopped flat-leaf parsley

¼ teaspoon fresh-ground black pepper

1. In a medium frying pan, heat the olive oil over moderately low heat. Add the garlic and the red-pepper flakes and cook, stirring, until the garlic softens, about 1 minute. Add the sliced mushrooms and the salt and cook until the mushrooms exude liquid, the liquid evaporates, and the mushrooms begin to brown, about 5 minutes.

2. In a large pot of boiling, salted water, cook the spaghettini until just done, about 9 minutes. Drain and toss with the mushroom mixture, the parsley, and the pepper.

VARIATIONS

SPAGHETTINI WITH GARLIC AND OIL

Eliminate the mushrooms and reduce the oil to 7 tablespoons. Just cook the garlic and red-pepper flakes for a minute and toss with the remaining ingredients.

SPAGHETTINI WITH WALNUTS, GARLIC, AND OIL

Eliminate the mushrooms and reduce the olive oil to 7 tablespoons. At the end, toss in ⅔ cup of toasted and chopped walnuts.

SPAGHETTINI WITH SALAMI, GARLIC, AND OIL

Eliminate the mushrooms and reduce the olive oil to 7 tablespoons. Cut ¼ pound of sliced salami into thin strips and toss it into the spaghettini with the parsley and black pepper.

PENNE WITH ROASTED MARSALA MUSHROOMS

The mushrooms are roasted until brown and then simmered in Marsala until they absorb the wine. A touch of tomato paste and chicken broth form a tasty sauce.

WINE RECOMMENDATION
Mushrooms are well matched with a red Italian wine such as a Nebbiolo d'Alba from the Piedmont region.

SERVES 4

- 1 pound mushrooms, cut in halves or quarters depending on size
- 2 tablespoons cooking oil
- ¾ teaspoon salt
- ½ teaspoon fresh-ground black pepper
- 2 cloves garlic, minced
- ¼ cup dry Marsala
- ½ cup canned low-sodium chicken broth or homemade stock
- 1 tablespoon tomato paste
- 1 tablespoon butter
- ¾ pound penne
- ¼ cup chopped fresh parsley

1. Heat the oven to 400°. In a roasting pan or dutch oven, toss the mushrooms with the oil and ¼ teaspoon each of the salt and pepper. Roast for 15 minutes; some liquid will remain in the pan.

2. Transfer the pan to the top of the stove. Stir in the garlic and Marsala. Simmer until the liquid is almost evaporated, about 4 minutes. Add the broth and tomato paste and simmer until about ¼ cup of liquid remains, about 2 minutes longer. Stir in the remaining ½ teaspoon salt and ¼ teaspoon pepper and the butter and remove from the heat.

3. In a large pot of boiling, salted water, cook the penne until just done, about 13 minutes. Drain the pasta and toss it with the sauce and the parsley.

VARIATION

PENNE WITH ROASTED MUSHROOMS
If you don't keep Marsala on hand, substitute an equal quantity of dry sherry or dry red wine in its place.

ZITI WITH PORTOBELLO MUSHROOMS, CARAMELIZED ONIONS, AND GOAT CHEESE

Meaty mushrooms are enhanced by sweet caramelized onions and just enough tangy melted goat cheese in this delicious year-round pasta.

WINE RECOMMENDATION
While the mushrooms need a red wine, the goat cheese goes best with a wine that has plenty of acidity. A pinot noir from Oregon is an ideal choice for both.

SERVES 4

2 tablespoons butter

4 tablespoons olive oil

3 onions, chopped

1 teaspoon salt

½ teaspoon sugar

1 pound portobello mushrooms, stems removed, caps halved and then cut crosswise into ¼-inch slices

3 tablespoons chopped fresh parsley

¼ teaspoon fresh-ground black pepper

¾ pound ziti

3 ounces soft goat cheese, such as Montrachet, crumbled

3 tablespoons grated Parmesan cheese, plus more for serving

1. In a large frying pan, melt 1 tablespoon of the butter with 2 tablespoons of the oil over moderate heat. Add the onions, ½ teaspoon of the salt, and the sugar and cook, stirring frequently, until the onions are well browned, about 20 minutes. Remove from the pan.

2. In the same pan, melt the remaining 1 tablespoon butter with 1 tablespoon of the oil over moderate heat. Add the mushrooms and ¼ teaspoon of the salt and cook, stirring occasionally, until tender and brown, about 8 minutes. Add the reserved onions, the parsley, the remaining ¼ teaspoon salt, and the pepper.

3. In a large pot of boiling, salted water, cook the ziti until just done, about 13 minutes. Reserve ¾ cup of the pasta water and drain. Toss the ziti and ½ cup of the reserved pasta water with the mushroom mixture, the remaining 1 tablespoon oil, the goat cheese, and the Parmesan. If the pasta seems dry, add more of the reserved pasta water. Serve with additional Parmesan.

SPAGHETTI WITH CREAMY SPINACH AND TARRAGON

Cream cheese melts in the heat of the pasta to form a luscious sauce. The fresh spinach called for here provides a delicate flavor that frozen spinach just doesn't duplicate. For speed, we recommend the prewashed kind available in supermarkets.

WINE RECOMMENDATION

Chenin blanc grapes make a wine that is fruity but bursting with acidity—an excellent match for tarragon. Try either a bottle of Vouvray from France or one of chenin blanc from California.

SERVES 4

- 10   ounces prewashed spinach
- 2   tablespoons butter
- 3   scallions including green tops, chopped
- 1½   teaspoons dried tarragon
- ¾   teaspoon salt
- ¾   pound spaghetti
- 5   ounces cream cheese, cut into cubes
- 2   tablespoons chopped fresh parsley
- ¼   cup grated Parmesan cheese
- ½   teaspoon fresh-ground black pepper

1. Remove any tough stems from the spinach. In a large frying pan, melt the butter over moderately low heat. Add the scallions and tarragon and cook for 2 minutes. Add the spinach and salt and stir until wilted. Simmer until the liquid evaporates from the spinach, about 5 minutes.

2. In a large pot of boiling, salted water, cook the spaghetti until just done, about 12 minutes. Reserve 1 cup of the pasta water. Drain the spaghetti and toss with ¾ cup of the reserved pasta water, the spinach mixture, the cream cheese, parsley, Parmesan, and pepper. If the sauce seems too thick, add more of the reserved pasta water.

SPINACH OPTIONS

You can buy fresh spinach in various forms, depending on how hard you want to work.

■ **Salad bar:** Weigh out 10 ounces of spinach from your supermarket's salad bar, and you're ready to cook—no rinsing or stem removal required.

■ **Prewashed bags:** Supermarkets carry 10-ounce bags of spinach. This has been cleaned of all visible sand, but we would still give it one final rinse before cooking.

■ **Bunches of fresh spinach:** You will need 1½ pounds to equal 10 ounces of packaged cleaned spinach. Remove the stems and then wash the leaves several times to get rid of the grit.

FETTUCCINE WITH SWISS CHARD AND DRIED FRUIT

The regrettably underused leafy vegetable Swiss chard makes an appearance here with apricots, currants, port, and pine nuts—altogether unexpected and delectable.

WINE RECOMMENDATION
A fruity white wine, such as a gewürztraminer or chenin blanc from California, will nicely echo the combination of fruit and spice.

SERVES 4

3   tablespoons pine nuts

5   tablespoons cooking oil

1   clove garlic, minced

2   bunches green or red Swiss chard, large stems removed, leaves washed and cut into 2-inch pieces (about 8 cups)

1½ teaspoons salt

¾   teaspoon fresh-ground black pepper

¼   cup sliced dried apricots

¼   cup currants or raisins

½   cup port

⅛   teaspoon cinnamon

¾   pound fettuccine

¼   cup grated Parmesan cheese

1. Heat the oven to 350°. Toast the pine nuts until golden brown, about 8 minutes.

2. In a large frying pan, heat the oil over moderately low heat. Add the garlic and cook for 30 seconds. Add the Swiss chard and ½ teaspoon each of the salt and pepper. Cook until the chard is wilted and most of the liquid is evaporated, about 3 minutes. Add the apricots, currants, port, and cinnamon and simmer until the port is reduced to about 2 tablespoons, 1 to 2 minutes. Remove from the heat.

3. In a large pot of boiling, salted water, cook the fettuccine until just done, about 12 minutes. Drain the pasta and toss it with the sauce, Parmesan, pine nuts, and the remaining 1 teaspoon salt and ¼ teaspoon pepper.

VARIATION

FETTUCCINE WITH SPINACH AND DRIED FRUIT

You can use spinach instead of the Swiss chard. Use 10 ounces of prewashed spinach or 1½ pounds in bunches.

FUSILLI WITH SUMMER TOMATO SAUCE

For this light, uncooked sauce, you must have perfectly ripe tomatoes. Be sure they're at room temperature, too, not cold. In fact, tomatoes shouldn't be refrigerated at all; chilling permanently reduces their flavor.

WINE RECOMMENDATION
Look for a simple, slightly acidic red wine to pair with the acidity of the tomatoes. Chianti and dolcetto, both from Italy, are good bets.

SERVES 4

2   pounds ripe tomatoes (about 4), chopped

1   large clove garlic, minced

3   tablespoons olive oil

1¼ teaspoons salt

¼   teaspoon fresh-ground black pepper

⅔   cup lightly packed fresh basil

1   pound fusilli

⅓   cup grated Parmesan cheese, plus more
    for serving

1. In a food processor or blender, combine the tomatoes, garlic, oil, salt, and pepper and puree. Add the basil and pulse just to mix.

2. In a large pot of boiling, salted water, cook the fusilli until just done, about 13 minutes. Drain the pasta and toss with the sauce and the Parmesan cheese. Let sit for about 1 minute to allow the pasta to absorb some of the liquid. Serve with additional Parmesan.

FRESH TOMATOES

We use plenty of canned tomatoes with pasta, but for this raw sauce, fresh, lusciously ripe specimens are essential. Take advantage of the abundant crop in August and September. If you live in an area with a farmers' market, or have a garden of your own, experiment with different types—red, yellow, orange, heirloom. Each of these has a unique flavor.

SPAGHETTI WITH TOMATOES, BLACK OLIVES, GARLIC, AND FETA CHEESE

Here's an ideal summer pasta with fresh tomatoes as the main attraction. Feta complements the tomatoes beautifully, and the heat of the pasta and hot garlic oil make the cheese meltingly soft.

WINE RECOMMENDATION

The saltiness of the olives and feta cheese and the acidity of the tomatoes make a refreshingly fruity red wine such as a Beaujolais-Villages the perfect thing to serve.

SERVES 4

1½ pounds tomatoes (about 3), seeded and cut into ½-inch pieces

½ cup Kalamata or other black olives, pitted

¼ pound feta cheese, crumbled

3 tablespoons drained capers

3 tablespoons chopped flat-leaf parsley

¼ teaspoon salt

¼ teaspoon fresh-ground black pepper

¾ pound spaghetti

6 tablespoons olive oil

3 cloves garlic, minced

1. In a large glass or stainless-steel bowl, combine the tomatoes, olives, feta, capers, parsley, salt, and pepper.

2. In a large pot of boiling, salted water, cook the spaghetti until just done, about 12 minutes. Drain.

3. Meanwhile, in a medium frying pan, heat the olive oil over moderately low heat. Add the garlic and cook, stirring, for 1 minute. Add the cooked pasta and the garlic oil to the tomato mixture and toss.

VARIATIONS

SPAGHETTI WITH TOMATOES, BLACK OLIVES, GARLIC, AND MOZZARELLA

Use ¾ pound fresh mozzarella cheese, cut into ¼-inch pieces, in place of the feta.

SPAGHETTI WITH TOMATOES, OLIVES, GARLIC, FETA, AND FRESH HERBS

Use ¼ cup chopped fresh basil or 3 tablespoons mixed chopped fresh herbs, such as tarragon and chives, in place of the parsley.

BOW TIES WITH SUN-DRIED TOMATO AND SCALLION CREAM

Sun-dried tomatoes give intense flavor to this quick, no-cook sauce. Fusilli would also be a good shape to use here; the cream sauce will cling to its every curve.

WINE RECOMMENDATION
A fruity red wine will be ideal with the rich sauce and the assertive, salty taste of the sun-dried tomatoes. A slightly chilled bottle of barbera or dolcetto from the Piedmont region of Italy would be perfect.

SERVES 4

5	scallions, white and light-green parts only
6	tablespoons chopped reconstituted sun-dried tomato halves (about 12 halves)
1	cup light cream or half-and-half
1	pound bow ties
1	teaspoon salt
1/2	teaspoon fresh-ground black pepper
3	tablespoons chopped fresh parsley

1. In a blender or food processor, puree the scallions and sun-dried tomatoes with 1/2 cup of the cream.

2. In a large pot of boiling, salted water, cook the bow ties until just done, about 15 minutes. Reserve 1/2 cup of the pasta water. Drain the pasta and toss with the puree, the remaining 1/2 cup cream, 1/3 cup of the reserved pasta water, the salt, pepper, and parsley. If the sauce seems too thick, thin it by adding more of the reserved pasta water.

VARIATION

BOW TIES WITH SUN-DRIED TOMATO AND HERB CREAM

An equal quantity of chopped fresh basil or chives or 2 tablespoons of tarragon would be a good alternative or addition to the parsley.

RECONSTITUTING SUN-DRIED TOMATOES

In a small pan, bring enough water to a boil to cover the dried tomatoes. Add the tomatoes, then remove from the heat and let steep in the hot water for about 5 minutes. Drain. You can also use drained oil-packed sun-dried tomatoes for this recipe. Since they're already soft, you don't have to reconstitute them.

SHELLS WITH GAZPACHO SAUCE AND AVOCADO

The bounty of late summer—tomatoes, red peppers, cucumber, and dill—goes into this refreshing sauce. The gazpacho is pureed in a food processor or blender, and so you don't need to spend a lot of time cutting the vegetables into neat dice the way you do for traditional gazpacho.

WINE RECOMMENDATION
Beer suits this dish better than any wine. Serve your own favorite or a cold, light Mexican beer such as Corona.

SERVES 4

½   cup chopped red onion
2   cloves garlic, smashed
1   jalapeño pepper, seeds and ribs removed
½   large red bell pepper, seeded
1   cucumber, peeled and seeded
1   pound plum tomatoes (about 5), seeded
1¾ teaspoons salt
½   teaspoon fresh-ground black pepper
¼   teaspoon ground cumin
¼   teaspoon wine vinegar
¼   cup dried breadcrumbs
¼   cup olive oil
2   tablespoons chopped fresh dill
1   avocado
¾   pound medium pasta shells

1. In a food processor or blender, combine the onion, garlic, jalapeño pepper, bell pepper, cucumber, tomatoes, salt, pepper, cumin, vinegar, and breadcrumbs. Pulse until chopped. With the machine running, add the oil in a thin stream. Add the dill and pulse once to combine. Dice the avocado and add it to the sauce.

2. In a large pot of boiling, salted water, cook the pasta until just done, about 10 minutes. Drain the pasta and toss with the sauce.

SPICING IT UP

If you like your gazpacho a little spicier, try one of these quick additions:
■ Leave some of the seeds in the jalapeño.
■ Add a dash of Tabasco sauce.
■ Add a pinch of cayenne.

PENNE WITH SALSA VERDE, MOZZARELLA, AND CHERRY TOMATOES

Piquant parsley-based salsa verde with its capers, anchovies, and vinegar is a perfect foil for chunks of mild mozzarella.

WINE RECOMMENDATION

Look for a white wine that goes well with the saltiness of the capers and anchovy paste and the acidity of the tomatoes. One from the south of France, such as an ugni blanc from the Côtes de Gascogne, will do nicely.

SERVES 4

- ¾ cup lightly packed flat-leaf parsley with thick stems removed
- 2 cloves garlic, smashed
- 1½ tablespoons drained capers
- ½ teaspoon anchovy paste
- 6 tablespoons olive oil
- ¾ teaspoon red-wine vinegar
- ¾ teaspoon salt
- ¼ teaspoon fresh-ground black pepper
- ¾ pound penne rigate
- ¾ pound fresh mozzarella, cut into ¼-inch cubes
- 2 cups cherry tomatoes, cut into quarters

1. In a blender or food processor, puree the parsley, the smashed garlic, the capers, and the anchovy paste with the olive oil, the wine vinegar, and the salt and pepper.

2. In a large pot of boiling, salted water, cook the penne rigate until just done, about 13 minutes. Drain.

3. In a large bowl, toss the pasta with the parsley mixture, mozzarella, and tomatoes.

FRESH MOZZARELLA

Fresh mozzarella is a soft, white cheese formed into a ball, which is usually packaged with water in plastic tubs to keep it moist. The cheese has a mild, milky taste that combines well with other, stronger flavors, and melts to a nice oozy texture. It's becoming more and more available in grocery stores; we have seen the Poly-O brand in many locations. Drain the cheese before using.

TEST-KITCHEN TIP

Cut the mozzarella into cubes first thing and let it sit at room temperature while you prepare the rest of the recipe. That way the mozzarella will melt more quickly.

MARINATED ZUCCHINI WITH BOW TIES

Garden-fresh zucchini and tomatoes make a beautiful pasta, perfect for a warm summer night's dinner. It can be served hot or at room temperature, either for four as a main course or for eight as a side dish—with grilled chicken, for instance.

WINE RECOMMENDATION
This dish puts one in mind of the French Mediterranean, and a red or white wine from that region would be a perfect accompaniment. Try a red from the Côtes de Provence or Bandol, a white from the town of Cassis, or even a rosé from the same area.

SERVES 4

1/3 cup plus 3 tablespoons olive oil

4 cloves garlic, minced

2 pounds zucchini (about 4), cut in half lengthwise and then cut crosswise into 1/4-inch slices

2 1/2 teaspoons salt

3/4 pound plum tomatoes (about 6), seeded and diced

1/2 cup chopped fresh basil

1/4 cup plus 1 tablespoon wine vinegar

1 1/2 teaspoons fresh-ground black pepper

1 pound bow ties

1. In a large frying pan, heat 3 tablespoons of the oil over moderate heat. Add the garlic, zucchini, and 1/2 teaspoon of the salt. Cook, stirring occasionally, until tender, about 5 minutes. Transfer the zucchini to a large stainless-steel, glass, or ceramic bowl and stir in the tomatoes, basil, vinegar, the remaining 2 teaspoons salt, and the pepper.

2. In a large pot of boiling, salted water, cook the bow ties until just done, about 15 minutes. Drain the pasta and toss it with the marinated zucchini and the remaining 1/3 cup oil.

VARIATION

BALSAMIC-MARINATED ZUCCHINI WITH BOW TIES

For a sweeter dish, you can substitute an equal amount of balsamic vinegar in place of the wine vinegar called for in the recipe.

ZITI WITH ROASTED VEGETABLES

Roasting vegetables at a high temperature caramelizes them, making them intensely flavorful. You may think of roasting as a long process, but we cut each of the vegetables into small cubes or thin slices so they need only thirty minutes in the oven.

WINE RECOMMENDATION
A dish such as this is reminiscent of the cuisine of Southern France, and a red wine from Provence, such as a Bandol or a Côtes de Provence, would make a good pairing.

SERVES 4

1 eggplant (about 1¼ pounds), cut into ½-inch cubes

2 zucchini, quartered lengthwise and then cut crosswise into ½-inch pieces

1 large red onion, quartered and cut into ¼-inch slices

4 tablespoons olive oil

¾ pound plum tomatoes (about 6), quartered

1¼ teaspoons salt

¾ pound ziti

2 tablespoons chopped fresh basil or parsley

1 tablespoon balsamic vinegar

¼ teaspoon fresh-ground black pepper

1. Heat the oven to 450°. In a large bowl, toss the eggplant, zucchini, and red onion with 2 tablespoons of the oil. Spread in a single layer on one large or two smaller baking sheets, preferably nonstick. Roast, stirring occasionally, until well browned and tender, about 30 minutes.

2. Meanwhile, place the tomatoes cut-side up in a small baking dish and sprinkle with ¼ teaspoon of the salt. Roast until soft, about 20 minutes. Transfer to a food processor or blender and puree.

3. In a large pot of boiling, salted water, cook the ziti until just done, about 12 minutes. Drain the pasta and toss with the tomato puree, the roasted vegetables, the basil, the remaining 2 tablespoons olive oil, the vinegar, the remaining 1 teaspoon salt, and the pepper.

VARIATION

ZITI WITH ROASTED VEGETABLES AND CHEESE

Add some crumbled goat cheese or grated Fontina when you toss the ziti. Or, put the finished pasta in an ovenproof baking dish, top with either of these two cheeses, and run it under the broiler until the cheese is golden brown.

GRILLED-VEGETABLE PASTA WITH CUMIN

If you're a fan of grilled vegetables, here's a fine way to turn them into a meal. We've selected a combination of eggplant, zucchini, and red bell pepper, but you can replace any of them with another vegetable, such as onions, tomatoes, or mushrooms.

WINE RECOMMENDATION
The fresh vegetables in this dish and the lemon juice should be matched with a lively, acidic white wine such as a sauvignon blanc. It's easy to find a Californian, but you might also try one from South Africa or New Zealand.

SERVES 4

1 small eggplant (about 1 pound), cut into ¼-inch rounds

2 small zucchini, cut lengthwise into ¼-inch slices

1 red bell pepper, quartered

1 clove garlic, minced

6 tablespoons olive oil

¾ teaspoon salt

¼ teaspoon fresh-ground black pepper

¼ teaspoon grated lemon zest

4 teaspoons lemon juice

3 tablespoons chopped fresh parsley

¾ teaspoon ground cumin

¾ pound penne rigate

   Grated Parmesan cheese, for serving

1. Light the grill or heat the broiler. In a large shallow bowl, toss the eggplant, zucchini, bell pepper, and garlic with 2 tablespoons of the oil, ¼ teaspoon of the salt, and ⅛ teaspoon of the black pepper. If using the broiler, arrange the vegetables in a single layer on one large or two smaller baking sheets, preferably nonstick. Grill or broil in batches, turning the vegetables once, until they are tender and lightly browned, 10 to 12 minutes. Cut the vegetables into 1½-inch pieces.

2. In a small glass or stainless-steel bowl, whisk together the remaining 4 tablespoons olive oil, the lemon zest, lemon juice, parsley, cumin, and the remaining ½ teaspoon salt and ⅛ teaspoon pepper.

3. In a large pot of boiling, salted water, cook the penne rigate until just done, about 13 minutes. Reserve about 3 tablespoons of the pasta water. Drain the penne and toss with 1 tablespoon of the reserved pasta water, the oil-and-lemon-juice mixture, and the vegetables. Add more pasta water if the pasta seems dry. Top with some Parmesan cheese and pass additional Parmesan at the table.

PENNE TRICOLORE

Zucchini, summer squash, and carrots are combined with Kalamata olives, basil, and plenty of lemon to make a delightful summery pasta. If you've got a garden full of zucchini, use twice as much and simply omit the summer squash. Then you can call the dish "Penne Duecolore."

WINE RECOMMENDATION
A crisp, quintessentially summer white wine, such as a fendant from Switzerland or an Orvieto or Soave from Italy, will accentuate the fresh basil and vegetables.

SERVES 4

¾ pound penne rigate

1 small zucchini, seeded and cut into 2-inch-long matchstick strips

1 small summer squash, seeded and cut into 2-inch-long matchstick strips

2 carrots, peeled and cut into 2-inch-long matchstick strips

½ cup Kalamata or other black olives, pitted

½ cup chopped fresh basil

¼ cup grated Parmesan cheese, plus more for serving

¼ cup olive oil

Grated zest from 1 lemon

1½ tablespoons lemon juice

½ teaspoon salt

¼ teaspoon fresh-ground black pepper

1. In a large pot of boiling, salted water, cook the penne rigate until almost done, about 11 minutes. Add the zucchini, summer squash, and carrots and bring back to a boil. Cook until the vegetables and penne are just done, about 2 minutes longer. Reserve ½ cup of the pasta water. Drain the penne and vegetables.

2. In a large bowl, toss the pasta, vegetables, 6 tablespoons of the reserved pasta water, olives, basil, Parmesan, oil, lemon zest, lemon juice, salt, and pepper. If the pasta seems dry, add more of the reserved pasta water. Serve with additional Parmesan.

SEEDING ZUCCHINI AND SUMMER SQUASH

Because the zucchini and summer squash are boiled in this recipe, it's a good idea to seed them first. Otherwise, the pulpy seeds get water-logged. To remove them, cut the zucchini or squash into quarters lengthwise. Then simply cut off the seeds.

MACARONI AND CHEESE

Even if you're not feeling nostalgic, you'll find this slightly updated version of an old favorite irresistible. And it's incredibly fast and easy because you don't have to make a sauce or even bake the macaroni.

WINE RECOMMENDATION
Don't uncork the rare vintage Bordeaux for this one! A simple, straightforward dish needs a wine with the same qualities. Find a Beaujolais-Villages from France or a California wine made from the fruit-filled gamay or mourvèdre grape and chill it before serving.

SERVES 4

¾ pound elbow macaroni

4 tablespoons butter

8 ounces sharp cheddar cheese, grated (about 2 cups)

1 tablespoon Dijon mustard

A few dashes of Tabasco sauce (optional)

½ teaspoon salt, or more to taste

⅛ teaspoon fresh-ground black pepper

1. In a large pot of boiling, salted water, cook the macaroni until just done, about 8 minutes. Drain and return to the hot pot.

2. Put the pot over the lowest possible heat and add the butter, cheese, mustard, Tabasco sauce if using, salt, and pepper. Stir until the cheese melts, and serve.

> ## TEST-KITCHEN TIP
>
> Pre-grated cheeses are certainly convenient, but what you gain in time you lose in taste. Since cheddar cheese is the star ingredient here, try to find one of excellent quality and grate it yourself. It takes only minutes on a hand-held grater. You can grate the cheese while the pasta is cooking. There are a number of delicious cheddars on the market, including those from Vermont, New York, Wisconsin, and Oregon. Either white or orange is fine.

ZITI WITH ROQUEFORT SAUCE

You'll want nothing more with this full-flavored pasta than a green salad or, in season, plain sliced tomatoes.

WINE RECOMMENDATION
Roquefort is tough to match with wine. We favor an acidic white, such as a chenin blanc from France's Loire Valley, or an acidic red, such as a young dolcetto from the Piedmont region in Italy.

SERVES 4

- 6 ounces Roquefort cheese
- 1½ cups heavy cream
- ½ cup canned low-sodium chicken broth or homemade stock
- ⅓ cup dry white wine
- 2 tablespoons butter
- ¾ teaspoon salt
- ¼ teaspoon fresh-ground black pepper
- ¾ pound ziti
- ¼ cup grated Parmesan cheese, plus more for serving
- 2 tablespoons chopped fresh parsley

1. In a medium bowl, mash the Roquefort with a fork. Add the cream a little at a time, whisking, until the mixture is fairly smooth. Some lumps of cheese will remain.

2. In a medium, stainless-steel saucepan, bring the chicken broth and the wine to a boil over moderate heat. Cook until reduced to ½ cup, about 5 minutes. Add the butter.

3. Reduce the heat to moderately low and add the Roquefort mixture. Cook, stirring, until the sauce thickens slightly, about 3 minutes. Add the salt and pepper.

4. In a large pot of boiling, salted water, cook the ziti until just done, about 12 minutes. Drain the pasta and toss with the Roquefort cream sauce, the Parmesan, and the parsley. Serve with additional Parmesan.

BAKED ZITI WITH PESTO

Because it's baked, this pasta takes a bit longer from kitchen to table than other dishes in this book. You'll find the preparation time, though, is just as short as that of any other recipe here.

WINE RECOMMENDATION
This boldly flavored dish needs a rustic red wine to stand up to it. A Salice Salentino from the south of Italy or a Corbières or Cahors from France will serve well.

SERVES 4

½ pound ziti

2 tablespoons cooking oil

1 onion, chopped

2 cloves garlic, minced

2 cups canned crushed tomatoes in thick puree

¼ teaspoon salt

1 bay leaf

½ teaspoon fresh-ground black pepper

1 cup ricotta cheese

1½ cups grated, packaged mozzarella cheese

⅓ cup grated Parmesan cheese

¼ cup store-bought or homemade pesto

1. Heat the oven to 350°. Oil an 8-by-8-inch baking dish.

2. In a large pot of boiling, salted water, cook the pasta for 7 minutes. It will be partially cooked. Drain. Rinse with cold water and drain again thoroughly.

3. In a medium saucepan, heat 1½ tablespoons of the oil over moderately low heat. Add the onion and cook, stirring occasionally, until translucent, about 5 minutes. Add the garlic and cook, stirring, for 30 seconds. Add the tomatoes, salt, and bay leaf. Bring to a simmer over moderate heat and cook until very thick, about 10 minutes. Stir in ¼ teaspoon of the pepper. Remove the bay leaf.

4. In a small bowl, combine the ricotta, 1 cup of the mozzarella, about half the Parmesan, the pesto, and the remaining ¼ teaspoon pepper.

5. Put half of the cooked pasta into the prepared baking dish and top with about a third of the tomato sauce. Spread the ricotta mixture on the sauce in an even layer. Cover with the remaining pasta and then the remaining sauce. Top with the remaining ½ cup mozzarella and the remaining Parmesan. Drizzle with the remaining ½ tablespoon oil. Bake until bubbling, about 30 minutes. Let sit 10 minutes before cutting.

CHEESE TORTELLINI WITH WALNUT PESTO

Here's one of the quickest pesto sauces you'll come across. It's a perfect match for cheese tortellini, but you can use other tortellini such as mushroom or meat instead. The pesto is also great with just about any plain pasta.

WINE RECOMMENDATION
Look for a crisp, acidic white wine to cut through the richness of the walnuts. A sauvignon blanc from either California or New Zealand would be suitable.

SERVES 4

- 1 cup walnuts
- 1/3 cup lightly packed flat-leaf parsley with thick stems removed
- 2 cloves garlic, smashed
- 3 tablespoons grated Parmesan cheese, plus more for serving
- 1/2 cup olive oil
- 1/2 teaspoon salt
- 1/4 teaspoon fresh-ground black pepper
- 1 pound fresh or frozen cheese tortellini
- 1 tablespoon butter

1. In a food processor or blender, pulse the walnuts, parsley, garlic, Parmesan, oil, salt, and pepper to a coarse puree.

2. In a large pot of boiling, salted water, cook the tortellini until just done, about 4 minutes for fresh and 12 minutes for frozen. Reserve 1/2 cup of the pasta water. Drain the tortellini.

Toss with 1/4 cup of the reserved pasta water, the walnut pesto, and the butter. If the pasta seems dry, add more of the reserved pasta water. Sprinkle with additional Parmesan and pass more at the table.

FRESH, FROZEN, AND DRIED TORTELLINI

We recommend fresh tortellini, which are sold in the refrigerator section of most supermarkets. Frozen are a close second and great to have on hand. Both of these are better than dried.

SPAGHETTI WITH PARSLEY ALMOND PESTO

Parsley, rather than the traditional basil, makes this pesto a year-round staple. Because the taste of almonds is more delicate than that of the usual pine nuts, we have chopped rather than ground them. Their flavor really comes through when you bite into a nutty chunk.

WINE RECOMMENDATION
With the parsley, olive oil, and almonds, a simple, lively white wine is best. Good examples are a pinot grigio from the Alto Adige and a Vernaccia di San Gimignano from Tuscany.

SERVES 4

1	clove garlic
1½	cups lightly packed flat-leaf parsley with thick stems removed
¾	teaspoon salt
⅓	cup olive oil
⅓	cup unsalted blanched almonds
¾	pound spaghetti
2	plum tomatoes, chopped

1. In a food processor, puree the garlic and parsley with the salt. With the machine running, add the olive oil in a thin stream. Add the almonds and pulse to chop.

2. In a large pot of boiling, salted water, cook the spaghetti until just done, about 12 minutes. Reserve ½ cup of the pasta water. Drain the spaghetti and toss with ¼ cup of the reserved pasta water, the pesto, and the tomatoes. If the sauce seems too thick, add more of the reserved pasta water.

VARIATIONS

SPAGHETTI WITH PARSLEY ALMOND PESTO AND PARMESAN

Stir ¼ cup grated Parmesan into the parsley pesto after chopping the almonds.

SPAGHETTI WITH PARSLEY PINE-NUT PESTO

Use ⅓ cup pine nuts in place of the almonds for a more traditional pesto.

WHAT IS PESTO?

Traditional pesto is an uncooked sauce from Genoa made with basil, garlic, olive oil, grated cheese, and pine nuts. More recently pesto, which literally means *crushed*, is being used as a general term to describe many herb-and-nut purees. Feel free to experiment with different herbs, nuts, and grated cheeses, depending on what you like and can get easily.

LINGUINE WITH GREMOLADA

Gremolada traditionally consists of minced garlic, parsley, and lemon zest. We've added lemon juice and orange zest to bring even more citrus flavor to the dish. The garlic here is raw and the quantity generous; feel free to cut back.

WINE RECOMMENDATION The acidity in this dish will pair well with a light, simple white wine. Among the many good choices are vinho verde from Portugal and fendant from Switzerland.

SERVES 4

Grated zest from 2 large lemons (about 2 teaspoons)

Grated zest from 1 orange (about 2 teaspoons)

4 cloves garlic, minced

1/3 cup chopped flat-leaf parsley

1 1/2 teaspoons lemon juice

3/4 teaspoon salt

1/4 teaspoon fresh-ground black pepper

1/2 cup olive oil

1 pound linguine

1. In a small glass or stainless-steel bowl, mix together the grated lemon and orange zests, the garlic, parsley, lemon juice, salt, pepper, and olive oil.

2. In a large pot of boiling, salted water, cook the linguine until just done, about 12 minutes. Drain and toss with the sauce.

VARIATIONS

LINGUINE WITH GREMOLADA AND CRAB

Toss 1/2 pound of lump crabmeat, picked free of any shell, with the linguine and the gremolada.

LINGUINE WITH GREMOLADA AND SHRIMP

Add 1/2 pound of peeled uncooked medium shrimp to the pasta during the last 1 minute of cooking time.

LINGUINE WITH GREMOLADA AND SCALLOPS

Season 1/2 pound of sea scallops with salt and pepper. Heat 1 tablespoon of cooking oil in a large, nonstick frying pan over moderately high heat and cook the scallops for 1 to 2 minutes per side. Top the pasta with the scallops.

Seafood
&
Poultry

PENNE WITH SHRIMP AND SPICY TOMATO SAUCE

Paprika, cumin, and ginger lend their aromatic alchemy to a simple, no-cook tomato sauce. You can use the sauce with a wide range of ingredients (see Variations).

WINE RECOMMENDATION
With its competing spices, strong-flavored cilantro, and acidic tomatoes, this pasta dish calls for a simple Italian white—a pinot grigio, for example.

SERVES 4

¼ cup olive oil

1 tablespoon lemon juice

1½ teaspoons paprika

1½ teaspoons ground cumin

¼ teaspoon ground ginger

¼ teaspoon dried oregano

½ teaspoon salt

⅛ teaspoon fresh-ground black pepper

¾ cup canned crushed tomatoes in thick puree

⅓ cup chopped cilantro or parsley

¾ pound penne rigate

1 pound medium shrimp, shelled

1. In a large glass or stainless-steel bowl, whisk together the olive oil and the lemon juice with the paprika, cumin, ginger, oregano, salt, and pepper. Stir in the crushed tomatoes and the cilantro.

2. In a large pot of boiling, salted water, cook the penne rigate until almost done, about 12 minutes. Add the shrimp and cook until it and the pasta are just done, about 1 minute longer. Drain. Toss with the tomato sauce.

VARIATIONS

PENNE WITH MOZZARELLA AND SPICY TOMATO SAUCE

Use 1 pound fresh mozzarella, cut into ¼-inch cubes, in place of the shrimp. Toss the cheese in at the end.

PENNE WITH SAUSAGE AND SPICY TOMATO SAUCE

Use grilled sausage cut into bite-size pieces in place of the shrimp. Toss the sausage into the pasta with the tomato sauce.

PENNE WITH GRILLED VEGETABLES AND SPICY TOMATO SAUCE

In place of the shrimp, use grilled or sautéed vegetables such as mushrooms, zucchini, eggplant, or green beans, cut into bite-size pieces. Toss the vegetables into the pasta with the sauce.

SHRIMP FRA DIAVOLO WITH VERMICELLI

The thin strands of pasta soak up this spicy tomato sauce to form a flavorful mound punctuated with shrimp.

WINE RECOMMENDATION
Look for a refreshing, fruity red to contrast with the heat of the red-pepper flakes. A bottle of food-friendly dolcetto or barbera from the Piedmont region of Italy would be perfect.

SERVES 4

2	tablespoons cooking oil
1	onion, chopped
2	cloves garlic, minced
1½	cups canned crushed tomatoes in thick puree (one 16-ounce can)
¼	teaspoon dried red-pepper flakes
¼	cup water
¼	cup chopped fresh parsley
¾	teaspoon salt
1	pound medium shrimp, shelled
¾	pound vermicelli

1. In a large frying pan, heat the oil over moderately low heat. Add the onion and cook, stirring occasionally, until translucent, about 5 minutes. Add the garlic and cook, stirring, 30 seconds longer. Stir in the tomatoes, red-pepper flakes, water, parsley, and salt. Reduce the heat and simmer, covered, for 10 minutes. Add the shrimp and cook, covered, just until the shrimp are pink, about 4 minutes.

2. In a large pot of boiling, salted water, cook the vermicelli until just done, about 9 minutes. Drain the pasta and toss with the tomato sauce and shrimp.

VARIATIONS

LOBSTER FRA DIAVOLO WITH VERMICELLI

If you're in a celebratory mood, lobster would taste great in place of the shrimp.

VERMICELLI FRA DIAVOLO

The full-flavored sauce can stand on its own without the shrimp. Add a sprinkling of Parmesan cheese.

ROTELLE AND SHRIMP WITH YOGURT DILL DRESSING

A refreshing combination of yogurt, cucumber, and dill completes this shrimp-laced pasta salad. If the pasta absorbs too much moisture while standing, just add a little more yogurt to make it saucy again.

WINE RECOMMENDATION
The acidity of the yogurt and the strong herbal qualities of the dill will pair well with a high-acid white wine such as a Muscadet de Sèvre-et-Maine from France. As an alternative, try a reasonably priced sparkling wine.

SERVES 4

2 tablespoons butter

2 cloves garlic, minced

1 pound medium shrimp, shelled

1½ teaspoons salt

¼ teaspoon fresh-ground black pepper

1½ cups plain yogurt

¼ cup mayonnaise (optional)

1 jalapeño pepper, seeds and ribs removed, minced

1 cucumber, peeled, seeded, and diced

3 tablespoons chopped fresh dill

3 scallions including green tops, chopped

¼ teaspoon paprika

¾ pound rotelle

1. In a medium frying pan, melt the butter over moderate heat. Stir in the garlic and then the shrimp, ¼ teaspoon of the salt, and the pepper. Cook, stirring, until the shrimp are just done, about 4 minutes. Remove from the pan and set aside to cool.

2. In a large bowl, combine the yogurt, the mayonnaise, if using, the jalapeño, cucumber, dill, scallions, paprika, and the remaining 1¼ teaspoons salt.

3. In a large pot of boiling, salted water, cook the rotelle until just done, about 12 minutes. Drain the pasta, rinse with cold water, and drain thoroughly. Toss with the yogurt sauce and the shrimp and garlic.

RINSING PASTA

Never rinse pasta that you will be saucing and serving right away. Cooked pasta is covered with a thin layer of starch that helps the sauce cling to it. If you're making a salad, however, it's better to rinse this starch off to avoid gumminess when the pasta cools.

LINGUINE, CRAB, AND AVOCADO WITH SCALLION VINAIGRETTE

A pastel scallion sauce dresses the delicate crabmeat and creamy avocado, making a wonderful, quick main dish that's also elegant enough to be a first course at your next dinner party. As an appetizer, it will serve six.

WINE RECOMMENDATION

An acidic white wine is best with both the tart vinaigrette and the rich avocado. A white from the Loire region in France such as Sancerre (sauvignon blanc grape) or Savennières (chenin blanc grape) is a good choice.

SERVES 4

- 2 teaspoons grated fresh ginger
- 2 teaspoons lemon juice
- 1½ tablespoons red- or white-wine vinegar
- 2 scallions, white and light-green parts chopped, dark-green tops sliced
- 1 teaspoon soy sauce
- ⅓ cup cooking oil
- ¾ teaspoon salt
- ½ teaspoon grated lemon zest (from about ½ lemon)
- 1 avocado, preferably Hass
- ¾ pound linguine
- ½ pound lump crabmeat, picked free of shell

1. In a blender, combine the ginger, lemon juice, vinegar, the chopped scallions, the soy sauce, oil, and ¼ teaspoon of the salt. Blend until smooth, then stir in the lemon zest. Cut the avocado into ½-inch dice and add to the scallion vinaigrette.

2. In a large pot of boiling, salted water, cook the linguine until just done, about 12 minutes. Drain the pasta and toss it with the vinaigrette and avocado and the remaining ½ teaspoon salt. Gently fold in the crabmeat. Sprinkle with the sliced scallion tops. Serve warm.

TEST-KITCHEN TIP

As soon as the avocado is diced, put it into the vinaigrette. The acidity of the lemon juice and the vinegar will keep the avocado from browning if dinner is delayed.

LINGUINE WITH CLAMS, BACON, AND TOMATO

Clams and bacon form a delectable union enhanced by wine-flavored tomato sauce. We recommend chopped clams, which are sold in refrigerated containers in many fish shops and at supermarkets, but you can also use good-quality canned clams.

WINE RECOMMENDATION

The full flavor of the clams and the acidity of the tomatoes are best with a straightforward, acidic white wine. The classic French shellfish wine is Muscadet de Sèvre-et-Maine.

SERVES 4

¼ pound sliced bacon, cut crosswise into ½-inch strips

3 cloves garlic, minced

½ cup dry white wine

1½ cups canned crushed tomatoes in thick puree (one 16-ounce can)

1 cup bottled clam juice

¾ pound chopped clams, drained (about 1½ cups)

⅓ cup chopped flat-leaf parsley

¾ teaspoon salt, more if needed

¼ teaspoon dried red-pepper flakes

¾ pound linguine

1. In a large stainless-steel frying pan, cook the strips of bacon over moderate heat until almost crisp. Remove the bacon with a slotted spoon. Pour off all but 2 tablespoons of the fat from the pan.

2. Reduce the heat to moderately low. Add the garlic and cook, stirring, for 30 seconds. Add the wine. Stir in the bacon, tomatoes, and clam juice and bring to a simmer. Cook, partially covered, for 10 minutes. Add the clams, parsley, salt, and red-pepper flakes and simmer for 30 seconds longer. Do not cook the clams too long or they will toughen. Taste the sauce and add more salt if needed.

3. In a large pot of boiling, salted water, cook the linguine until just done, about 12 minutes. Drain the pasta and return it to the hot pot. Add the sauce and let sit 2 to 3 minutes so that the pasta absorbs some of the liquid.

Bow-Tie Salad with Scallops, Black Olives, Oranges, and Mint

Here's a unique and refreshing pasta salad with flavors reminiscent of Morocco and Southern Italy, where oranges and black olives are often paired.

WINE RECOMMENDATION
A white or rosé wine from Provence or the Languedoc-Roussillon region of France makes sense with this; either will pair well with the mint and the salty olive tastes of the dish.

SERVES 4

¾ pound bow ties

1 pound sea scallops

¾ teaspoon salt

¼ teaspoon fresh-ground black pepper

5 tablespoons olive oil

2 navel oranges

1 tablespoon lemon juice

½ cup Kalamata or other black olives, pitted

½ small red onion, chopped fine

6 tablespoons chopped fresh mint

1. In a large pot of boiling, salted water, cook the bow ties until just done, about 15 minutes. Drain, rinse with cold water, and drain thoroughly.

2. Meanwhile, season the scallops with ¼ teaspoon of the salt and ⅛ teaspoon of the pepper. In a large nonstick frying pan, heat 1 table-spoon of the oil over moderately high heat. Sear the scallops, in two batches if necessary, until brown and just done, 1 to 2 minutes per side. Let cool.

3. Using a stainless-steel knife, peel the oranges down to the flesh, removing all of the white pith. Cut the sections away from the membranes and put them in a large glass or stainless-steel bowl. Squeeze the juice from the membranes into the bowl. Add the remaining 4 tablespoons oil, the lemon juice, olives, onion, mint, and the remaining ½ teaspoon salt and ⅛ teaspoon pepper. Stir to combine. Add the pasta and scallops and stir again.

LINGUINE PICCOLE WITH GRILLED SWORDFISH AND PARSLEY ANCHOVY SAUCE

Don't let a fear of anchovies keep you from this delicious dish. They give a roundness and depth of flavor rather than a strong hit of anchovy.

WINE RECOMMENDATION
A dry rosé wine would go nicely with the anchovy sauce. Look for a bottle from either Provence in France or, if you're feeling adventurous, Navarre in Spain.

SERVES 4

1   small shallot, peeled, or 2 scallions, chopped

8   flat anchovy fillets, or 2 teaspoons anchovy paste

2   tablespoons red-wine vinegar

½   teaspoon lemon juice

1   tablespoon grated Parmesan cheese

¾   teaspoon salt

½   teaspoon fresh-ground black pepper

½   cup plus 1 teaspoon olive oil

2   tablespoons hot water

1   pound swordfish steak, about 1 inch thick

½   pound thin linguine, such as linguine piccole or linguine fini

⅓   cup chopped fresh parsley

1. In a blender, combine the shallot, anchovies, vinegar, lemon juice, Parmesan, ½ teaspoon of the salt, and ¼ teaspoon of the pepper. Blend to form a paste. While the machine is running, add the ½ cup oil in a thin stream and then add the hot water.

2. Heat the broiler or a grill pan, or light the grill. Coat the swordfish with the 1 teaspoon oil and sprinkle with the remaining ¼ teaspoon salt and ¼ teaspoon pepper. Cook the fish for 4 minutes. Turn and cook until golden brown and just done, 4 to 5 minutes longer. Let the fish rest for a few minutes and then cut it into bite-size pieces.

3. In a large pot of boiling, salted water, cook the linguine piccole until just done, about 9 minutes. Reserve about ½ cup of the pasta water. Drain the pasta and toss with the sauce, the swordfish, ¼ cup of the reserved pasta water, and the parsley. If the sauce seems too thick, add more of the reserved water.

VARIATION

LINGUINE PICCOLE WITH TUNA AND PARSLEY ANCHOVY SAUCE
Drain one 6-ounce can of tuna packed in oil. Flake the tuna and toss it with the drained pasta in place of the swordfish.

ZITI WITH HONEY MUSTARD SALMON

The salmon here is roasted with a thin coat of honey and a sprinkling of pepper and then tossed with the pasta and a subtle mustard cream sauce. For a more intense mustard flavor, add an additional teaspoon to the sauce.

WINE RECOMMENDATION
With the sweetness of the honey and the heat and acidity of the mustard, a fruity red wine such as a slightly chilled California pinot noir would be an excellent choice.

SERVES 4

  1   pound salmon fillet

  1   tablespoon honey

  ½   teaspoon fresh-ground black pepper

  1   tablespoon cooking oil

  1   onion, chopped

  ⅓   cup dry white wine

  1   teaspoon grainy or Dijon mustard

  ¾   cup heavy cream

1¼   teaspoons salt

  2   tablespoons chopped fresh parsley

  ¾   pound ziti

1. Heat the oven to 400°. Lightly oil a small roasting pan. Put the salmon in the pan, skin side down. Spread the honey over the salmon and then sprinkle with ¼ teaspoon of the pepper. Roast the salmon until just barely done, about 12 minutes, depending upon the thickness of the fillet. Remove from the oven.

2. In a medium saucepan, heat the oil over moderately low heat. Add the onion and cook, stirring occasionally, until translucent, about 5 minutes. Add the wine and simmer until about 1 tablespoon remains, about 2 minutes. Whisk in the mustard, cream, salt, and the remaining ¼ teaspoon pepper. Turn off the heat. Flake the salmon and stir it and the parsley into the sauce.

3. In a large pot of boiling, salted water, cook the ziti until just done, about 13 minutes. Drain the pasta and toss with the sauce.

LINGUINE WITH SEARED TUNA AND GREEN-OLIVE TAPENADE

Small pitted green olives—the bottled martini type—are transformed into a savory sauce in next to no time. We like the tuna rare, but if you prefer it well done, cook it a few minutes longer.

WINE RECOMMENDATION
The richness of the tuna and the saltiness of the tapenade are delightful accompanied by a light, fruity red—a Côtes-du-Rhône from Southern France or a barbera from Italy.

SERVES 4

½ cup pitted green olives

⅓ cup lightly packed flat-leaf parsley with thick stems removed

1 clove garlic, smashed

½ teaspoon anchovy paste

7 tablespoons olive oil

1½ teaspoons lemon juice

½ teaspoon salt

½ teaspoon fresh-ground black pepper

1 pound tuna steak, about 2 inches thick, cut into 3-inch squares

¾ pound linguine

1. In a food processor or blender, pulse the olives, parsley, and garlic to a coarse puree with the anchovy paste, 6 tablespoons of the olive oil, the lemon juice, and ¼ teaspoon each of the salt and pepper. Put three-quarters of the mixture in a large bowl.

2. Heat a grill pan or heavy frying pan over moderate heat. Coat the tuna with the remaining 1 tablespoon oil and season with the remaining ¼ teaspoon salt and ¼ teaspoon pepper. Cook about 1½ minutes per side. Remove the tuna. Let sit for 3 minutes. The fish will be rare. Cut it into ¼-inch slices.

3. In a large pot of boiling, salted water, cook the linguine until just done, about 12 minutes. Reserve about ½ cup of the pasta water. Drain the linguine, add it and ¼ cup of the reserved pasta water to the bowl with the olive mixture, and toss. If the sauce seems too thick, add more of the reserved pasta water. Mound the pasta on plates and top with the tuna. Spoon the remaining olive mixture on top.

SPAGHETTI WITH TUNA AND FRESH TOMATO SAUCE

Raw tomato sauce with loads of basil can be tossed together in just minutes. Add spaghetti and canned tuna and you have a fine summer meal.

WINE RECOMMENDATION
Look for an acidic and intensely flavored white wine, such as a grassy sauvignon blanc from California, to match the aggressive taste of the tuna.

SERVES 4

1½ pounds tomatoes (about 3), cut into approximately ½-inch dice

6 tablespoons olive oil

2 cloves garlic, minced

¾ cup chopped fresh basil

2 teaspoons balsamic or red-wine vinegar

1 teaspoon salt

½ teaspoon fresh-ground black pepper

¾ pound spaghetti

Two 6-ounce cans tuna packed in oil, drained

1. In a large bowl, combine the tomatoes, oil, garlic, basil, vinegar, salt, and pepper.

2. In a large pot of boiling, salted water, cook the spaghetti until just done, about 12 minutes. Drain and toss the pasta with the tuna and the tomato mixture.

VARIATIONS

SPAGHETTI WITH FRESH TOMATO SAUCE

Omit the tuna. The marinated tomatoes make a delicious sauce on their own.

SPAGHETTI WITH SALMON AND FRESH TOMATO SAUCE

Omit the tuna. Coat 1 pound of skinless salmon fillets with 1 tablespoon cooking oil and sprinkle with ¼ teaspoon salt and ⅛ teaspoon fresh-ground black pepper. Broil the salmon until just barely done, 3 to 5 minutes, depending on the thickness of the fillet. Flake the salmon and toss with the pasta.

SPAGHETTI WITH SHRIMP AND FRESH TOMATO SAUCE

Omit the tuna. Add 1 pound of raw medium shelled shrimp to the spaghetti during the last 1 minute of cooking time.

FEDELINI WITH TUNA AND CHICKPEAS

Fennel and orange zest complement one another as well as the pantry staples canned tuna, chickpeas, and tomatoes. If you don't happen to have fedelini on hand, spaghettini or vermicelli would be fine.

WINE RECOMMENDATION
Wine with plenty of acidity will stand up to the fennel and tuna. A bottle of either Sancerre from the Loire Valley in France or sauvignon blanc from California will do nicely.

SERVES 4

2   tablespoons cooking oil

1   small onion, cut into thin slices

¾   teaspoon fennel seeds

   Grated zest from ½ orange

1½   teaspoons salt

¼   teaspoon fresh-ground black pepper

1   cup canned crushed tomatoes

1   6-ounce can tuna packed in oil

1⅔   cups canned drained chickpeas (one 15-ounce can), rinsed

¾   pound fedelini

¼   cup chopped fresh parsley

1. In a large frying pan, heat the oil over moderately low heat. Add the onion and cook, stirring occasionally, until translucent, about 5 minutes. Add the fennel seeds, the orange zest, and the salt and pepper. Cook, stirring, for 1 minute longer. Add the tomatoes and simmer, covered, for 10 minutes. Add the tuna and its oil and the chickpeas, cover, and remove the pan from the heat.

2. In a large pot of boiling, salted water, cook the fedelini until just done, about 6 minutes. Reserve about ½ cup of the pasta water. Drain the pasta and toss with the sauce, ¼ cup of the reserved pasta water, and the parsley. If the sauce seems too thick, add more of the reserved pasta water.

CANNED TUNA

Different brands of tuna vary tremendously. Here we use tuna packed in oil, and we count on that oil as part of the sauce. If your tuna has less than 1½ tablespoons oil per can, add a little extra cooking oil to make up for the difference.

Bow Ties with Chicken, Watercress, and Walnuts

Chicken and walnuts always taste great together. Here the combination is enhanced by the peppery bite of watercress.

WINE RECOMMENDATION
This simple, flexible dish can go with either a red or a white wine. For a red, try a Beaujolais-Villages from France. If you prefer a white wine, look for something equally simple and fruity, such as an Albariño from Spain.

SERVES 4

- ⅓ cup walnuts
- 8 tablespoons olive oil
- 4 boneless, skinless chicken breasts (about 1⅓ pounds in all)

  Salt

  Fresh-ground black pepper
- 2 tablespoons red-wine vinegar
- ½ pound multicolored or plain bow ties
- 1 bunch watercress (about 5 ounces), large stems removed

1. In a large nonstick frying pan, toast the walnuts over moderate heat, stirring, until lightly browned, about 5 minutes. Remove the nuts from the pan and chop.

2. In the same pan, heat 2 tablespoons of the oil over moderate heat. Season the chicken breasts with ⅛ teaspoon each salt and pepper.

Cook the breasts until browned and just done, 4 to 5 minutes per side. Remove the chicken from the pan and let rest for 5 minutes before cutting the meat into chunks.

3. In a medium glass or stainless-steel bowl, combine the remaining 6 tablespoons oil, the vinegar, ¾ teaspoon salt, and ¼ teaspoon pepper. Add the chicken.

4. In a large pot of boiling, salted water, cook the bow ties until just done, about 15 minutes. Drain the pasta and toss it with the walnuts, the chicken-and-vinaigrette mixture, and the watercress. Serve warm.

GRILLED-CHICKEN PASTA SALAD WITH ARTICHOKE HEARTS

Using canned artichoke hearts cuts the preparation time for this salad way down. They are surprisingly good; just be sure to rinse them thoroughly to get rid of any extra acidity or "tinny" taste.

WINE RECOMMENDATION

Artichokes can be tough on wine since they tend to make even the driest ones taste sweet. To counteract this tendency, try an acidic white wine such as a Sancerre from France (made from sauvignon blanc grapes) or a sauvignon blanc from northern Italy.

SERVES 4

- 3 boneless, skinless chicken breasts (about 1 pound in all)
- 7 tablespoons olive oil
- 1¼ teaspoons salt
- ½ teaspoon fresh-ground black pepper
- ¾ pound fusilli
- 1¼ cups canned, drained artichoke hearts (one 14-ounce can), rinsed and cut into 6 wedges each
- 3 scallions including green tops, chopped
- ¼ cup chopped flat-leaf parsley
- 1 tablespoon red-wine vinegar
- 2 tablespoons grated Parmesan cheese

1. Light the grill or heat the broiler. Coat the chicken with 1 tablespoon of the oil and season with ¼ teaspoon of the salt and ¼ tea-spoon of the pepper. Grill or broil until just done, 4 to 5 minutes per side. Let the chicken rest for 5 minutes and then cut crosswise into ¼-inch slices.

2. In a large pot of boiling, salted water, cook the fusilli until just done, about 13 minutes. Drain, rinse with cold water, and drain thoroughly. In a large bowl, toss the pasta with 1 tablespoon of the olive oil.

3. Add the chicken, artichoke hearts, scallions, parsley, the remaining 5 tablespoons oil, the vinegar, the remaining 1 teaspoon salt and ¼ teaspoon pepper, and the Parmesan to the pasta and toss well.

FETTUCCINE WITH CHICKEN, SPINACH, AND CREAMY ORANGE SAUCE

Just one tablespoon of cream per person gives this fettuccine a luxurious taste and texture.

WINE RECOMMENDATION

A zippy white wine with good acidity will pair nicely with the spinach and orange flavors. Look for an Italian Arneis or a pinot grigio from the Collio region. Or, for something completely different, select a white Graves from France.

SERVES 4

- 2 tablespoons cooking oil
- 4 boneless, skinless chicken thighs (about 1 pound in all), cut into 1/4-inch strips
- 1 1/4 teaspoons salt
- 1/2 teaspoon fresh-ground black pepper
- 10 ounces prewashed spinach
- 2 cloves garlic, minced
- 1/2 pound mushrooms, sliced
- 1/2 teaspoon grated orange zest
- 1 tablespoon orange juice
- 1/4 cup canned low-sodium chicken broth or homemade stock
- 1/4 cup heavy cream
- 1/2 pound fettuccine

1. In a large nonstick frying pan, heat 1 tablespoon of the oil over moderately high heat. Season the chicken with 1/4 teaspoon each of the salt and pepper. Sauté until just cooked through, 2 to 3 minutes. Remove from the pan.

2. Remove any tough stems from the spinach. In the same pan used for the chicken, heat the remaining 1 tablespoon oil over moderate heat. Add the garlic and mushrooms and cook, stirring, for 2 minutes. Add the spinach, let it wilt, and stir in 1/2 teaspoon of the salt and the remaining 1/4 teaspoon pepper. Simmer for 2 minutes. Add the zest, orange juice, and chicken broth. Simmer for 2 minutes and then add the cream, the chicken, and the remaining 1/2 teaspoon salt. Remove from the heat.

3. In a large pot of boiling, salted water, cook the fettuccine until just done, about 12 minutes. Drain the pasta and toss with the chicken and sauce.

GREEK ZITI

You'll find an interesting technique here that guarantees juicy chicken: The boneless meat is steamed to moist perfection in hot chicken broth—off the heat.

■ WINE RECOMMENDATION
The acidity of the feta cheese and the lemon juice in this dish will work best with a light, fruity, just plain gulpable red wine. If you're feeling adventurous, try a Greek one such as Demestica.

SERVES 4

1 cup canned low-sodium chicken broth or homemade stock

2 teaspoons dried oregano

3 boneless, skinless chicken breasts (about 1 pound in all), cut into ½-inch cubes

½ pound ziti

4 ounces feta cheese, crumbled (about ¾ cup)

1 tablespoon lemon juice

1 teaspoon salt

½ teaspoon fresh-ground black pepper

3 tablespoons chopped fresh parsley

1½ cups cherry tomatoes, halved

1. In a large frying pan, simmer the chicken broth and the oregano until ½ cup of liquid remains in the pan, about 4 minutes. Stir in the chicken cubes, cover the pan, and remove it from the heat. Let the chicken steam in the hot broth until just done, about 8 minutes.

2. In a large pot of boiling, salted water, cook the ziti until just done, about 13 minutes. Drain the pasta and toss it with the chicken mixture, the feta, lemon juice, salt, pepper, and parsley. Stir until the cheese is completely melted. Toss in the cherry tomatoes.

PASTA SHELLS WITH CHICKEN AND BRUSSELS SPROUTS

If you've always thought that you dislike Brussels sprouts, you've probably never tried them in a combination like this. Mild chicken tames the strength of the sprouts while garlic, lemon juice, red-pepper flakes, and Parmesan unite the two main ingredients and complement them both. Frozen Brussels sprouts are surprisingly good in this recipe, too, though not as fine as fresh.

WINE RECOMMENDATION
A crisp white wine such as a chardonnay-based Chablis from France matches up nicely with the acidity of the lemon juice in the sauce.

SERVES 4

2 tablespoons cooking oil

3 tablespoons butter

4 boneless, skinless chicken breasts (about 1⅓ pounds in all)

1 teaspoon salt

½ teaspoon fresh-ground black pepper

½ red onion, chopped

2 cloves garlic, chopped

¾ pound fresh Brussels sprouts (or one 10-ounce package frozen), cut into quarters from top to stem end

1 cup canned low-sodium chicken broth or homemade stock

⅛ teaspoon dried red-pepper flakes

1½ teaspoons lemon juice

¼ cup chopped fresh parsley

⅓ cup grated Parmesan cheese

½ pound medium pasta shells

1. In a large nonstick frying pan, heat 1 tablespoon each of the oil and the butter over moderate heat. Season the chicken with ¼ teaspoon each of the salt and pepper. Cook the breasts until browned and just done, 4 to 5 minutes per side. Remove the chicken from the pan and let it rest for 5 minutes. Cut into small pieces.

2. In the same pan, heat the remaining 1 tablespoon oil over moderately low heat. Add the red onion and cook, stirring occasionally, until starting to soften, about 3 minutes. Stir in the garlic, Brussels sprouts, broth, and red-pepper flakes. Bring to a simmer and cook, covered, until the Brussels sprouts are just done, about 5 minutes. Add the chicken, lemon juice, parsley, Parmesan, and the remaining 2 tablespoons butter, ¾ teaspoon salt, and ¼ teaspoon pepper. Remove from the heat.

3. In a large pot of boiling, salted water, cook the pasta until just done, about 10 minutes. Drain and toss with the sauce.

CURRIED CHICKEN WITH APPLE OVER VERMICELLI

Here is a curry that can be made at home without a special trip for hard-to-find ingredients. We tested it using both coconut milk and cream; the results were equally tasty.

WINE RECOMMENDATION
This example of fusion cuisine (Indian-Thai-Italian) pairs well with a kabinett riesling from Germany's Mosel-Saar-Ruwer region. Don't be put off by the wine's slight residual sugar—it's a perfect foil for the flavors of the dish.

SERVES 4

- 2 tablespoons cooking oil
- 1 onion, chopped
- 2 cloves garlic, minced
- 1 tablespoon chopped fresh ginger
- 1 jalapeño pepper, seeds and ribs removed, chopped
- 1 tablespoon curry powder
- ¾ cup canned low-sodium chicken broth or homemade stock
- 4 boneless, skinless chicken breasts (about 1⅓ pounds in all), cut into ½-inch cubes
- 1 apple, preferably Granny Smith, peeled, cored, and diced
- 2 plum tomatoes, seeded and chopped
- ¼ cup canned unsweetened coconut milk or heavy cream
- ½ teaspoon salt
- 2 tablespoons chopped cilantro (optional)
- ½ pound vermicelli

1. In a large nonstick frying pan, heat the oil over moderately low heat. Add the onion and sauté, stirring occasionally, until it begins to soften, about 3 minutes. Add the garlic, ginger, and jalapeño and cook, stirring, for 1 minute longer. Stir in the curry powder and then the chicken broth. Bring the liquid to a simmer. Stir in the cubed chicken, cover the pan, and remove it from the heat. Let the chicken steam in the hot broth until almost done, about 5 minutes. Add the apple, tomatoes, coconut milk, salt, and the cilantro, if using. Simmer gently until the sauce thickens slightly, about 3 minutes.

2. In a large pot of boiling, salted water, cook the vermicelli until just done, about 9 minutes. Drain the pasta and toss with the curry sauce.

SPAGHETTI WITH CHICKEN AND THAI PEANUT SAUCE

A Thai favorite, peanut sauce flavored with soy, ginger, lime, and hot pepper is usually served as a dip alongside chicken or pork satay. In this version, East meets West; the sauce is thinned with chicken stock and tossed with spaghetti, chicken, and scallions.

WINE RECOMMENDATION
A little bit of sweetness in the wine would be great with the Asian spices here. A kabinett riesling from the Mosel-Saar-Ruwer region of Germany has just the touch and good acidity.

SERVES 4

- 3 tablespoons plus 1 teaspoon soy sauce
- 2 tablespoons plus 2 teaspoons lime juice (from about 2 limes)
- 1 tablespoon cooking oil, plus 1 tablespoon more if needed
- 4 cloves garlic, minced
- 3/4 teaspoon ground ginger
- 3 boneless, skinless chicken breasts (about 1 pound in all)
- 1/2 cup chunky peanut butter, preferably natural
- 1 cup canned low-sodium chicken broth or homemade stock
- 1/2 teaspoon sugar
- 1/2 teaspoon salt
- 1/8 teaspoon dried red-pepper flakes, or to taste
- 3/4 pound spaghetti
- 3 scallions including green tops, chopped
- 1/3 cup chopped peanuts (optional)

1. In a medium, shallow glass dish or stainless-steel pan, combine the 3 tablespoons soy sauce, the 2 tablespoons lime juice, 1 tablespoon of the oil, the garlic, and the ginger. Add the chicken; turn to coat. Let marinate at least 10 minutes.

2. Meanwhile, in a medium, stainless-steel saucepan, combine the remaining 1 teaspoon soy sauce and 2 teaspoons lime juice, the peanut butter, broth, sugar, salt, and red-pepper flakes. Pour the marinade from the chicken into the saucepan and bring just to a simmer over moderate heat, whisking until smooth.

3. Heat a grill pan over moderate heat. Cook the chicken until browned and just done, 4 to 5 minutes per side. Remove the chicken from the pan and let it rest for 5 minutes. Cut crosswise into 1/4-inch slices. Alternatively, heat the remaining 1 tablespoon oil in a heavy frying pan. Cook and slice the chicken in the same way.

4. In a large pot of boiling, salted water, cook the spaghetti until just done, about 12 minutes. Drain the pasta and toss with the peanut sauce, chicken, and scallions. Top with the chopped peanuts, if using.

PENNE WITH CHICKEN, GREEN BEANS, AND CASHEW BUTTER

Compound butter—a softened butter mixed with nuts, herbs, or any flavoring ingredient—is a simple base for creating a delicious sauce.

WINE RECOMMENDATION
A rich white wine, for example a chardonnay from California or Australia, will go particularly well with the richness of the cashews and butter.

SERVES 4

½ cup roasted cashews

6 tablespoons butter, softened

1 tablespoon cooking oil

4 boneless, skinless chicken breasts (about 1⅓ pounds in all)

¾ teaspoon salt

¾ teaspoon fresh-ground black pepper

¾ pound penne

½ pound green beans, cut into 1-inch lengths

1. Combine the cashews and the butter in a food processor. Pulse to a smooth paste. Or, finely chop the cashews and combine them with the butter.

2. In a medium nonstick frying pan, heat the oil over moderate heat. Season the chicken breasts with ¼ teaspoon each salt and pepper and add them to the pan. Cook until browned and just done, 4 to 5 minutes per side. Remove the chicken from the pan and let it rest for 5 minutes. Cut into small pieces.

3. In a large pot of boiling, salted water, cook the penne until just done, about 13 minutes. Add the beans during the last 5 minutes of cooking. Drain the pasta and beans and toss with the cashew butter, chicken, and the remaining ½ teaspoons of salt and pepper.

OTHER NUT BUTTERS

Cashews taste delicious in this dish, but you could really use any kind of nut, salted or unsalted, you have on hand. Others that would work:

- Almonds
- Hazelnuts
- Peanuts
- Pecans
- Pistachios
- Walnuts

PENNE WITH TURKEY, ARUGULA, AND SUN-DRIED-TOMATO VINAIGRETTE

Peppery arugula adds a distinctive bite to this appealing dish, but if arugula is unavailable, you can substitute watercress with similar results.

WINE RECOMMENDATION
A fruity red will complement the sharpness of the arugula. Try a Beaujolais-Villages from France or a dolcetto from Italy. In either case, chill the wine slightly before serving.

SERVES 4

6   reconstituted sun-dried tomato halves, chopped (see "Reconstituting Sun-Dried Tomatoes," page 47)

2   cloves garlic, smashed

1½ tablespoons balsamic vinegar

¾   teaspoon salt

½   teaspoon fresh-ground black pepper

⅓   cup plus 1 tablespoon olive oil

1   pound turkey cutlets, cut into ½-by-1½-inch strips

6   ounces arugula (about 3 bunches), cut into ½-inch strips, or 5 ounces (1 bunch) watercress, large stems removed

½   pound penne

1. In a blender, combine the sun-dried tomatoes, garlic, vinegar, ½ teaspoon of the salt, and ¼ teaspoon of the pepper. Blend until a paste forms. With the machine running, add the ⅓ cup oil in a thin stream.

2. Sprinkle the turkey with the remaining ¼ teaspoon each of the salt and pepper. In a large frying pan, heat the remaining 1 tablespoon oil over moderate heat. Cook the turkey, in two batches if necessary, until just cooked through, about 3 minutes. Do not overcook. Transfer the turkey to a large bowl and add the arugula.

3. In a large pot of boiling, salted water, cook the penne until just done, about 13 minutes. Drain, toss with the turkey and arugula and the tomato vinaigrette, and serve warm.

EGG NOODLES WITH TURKEY, BACON, AND ROSEMARY

Old-fashioned egg noodles are as good as ever. Here they're paired with quick cooking turkey cutlets—a real convenience food. The salty bacon helps bring out the flavor of the mild turkey. And rosemary enhances them both.

WINE RECOMMENDATION
The rosemary in this dish will go well with a light French red wine, such as a Côtes-du-Rhône. Or try a moderately priced California cabernet sauvignon.

SERVES 4

¼ pound sliced bacon, cut crosswise into ½-inch strips

1 pound turkey cutlets, cut into ½-by-1½-inch strips

¾ teaspoon salt

½ teaspoon fresh-ground black pepper

10 ounces prewashed spinach

½ cup canned low-sodium chicken broth or homemade stock

¾ teaspoon dried rosemary, crumbled

½ pound wide egg noodles

1 tablespoon butter, at room temperature

1. In a large frying pan, cook the bacon, stirring occasionally, until golden brown and just crisp, about 5 minutes. Remove and drain on paper towels. Pour off all but 2 tablespoons of the fat from the pan.

2. Heat the remaining bacon fat over moderately high heat. Sprinkle the turkey with ¼ teaspoon each of the salt and pepper. Add the turkey to the pan, in two batches if necessary, and cook, stirring frequently, until golden brown and just cooked through, about 3 minutes. Transfer to a plate.

3. Remove any tough stems from the spinach. Add the broth, rosemary, and the remaining ½ teaspoon salt to the pan and bring to a simmer, stirring to dislodge any brown bits that cling to the bottom of the pan. Add the spinach and cook, stirring, just until wilted, 1 to 2 minutes.

4. In a large pot of boiling, salted water, cook the noodles until just done, about 3 minutes. Drain. Add the noodles, butter, and the remaining ¼ teaspoon pepper to the frying pan and stir until the butter melts. Stir in the turkey with any accumulated juices and the bacon.

SPAGHETTI WITH SMOKED TURKEY AND LEEKS

Deli turkey goes upscale. This recipe is also a good place to use leftover turkey or roast chicken. Ham tastes great here, also.

WINE RECOMMENDATION
The smokiness of the turkey will be best with a red or white wine with lots of acidity. For a red, look for a pinot noir from Oregon. For a white, try a riesling from the Alsace region of France.

SERVES 4

1 tablespoon butter

3 large leeks, white and light-green parts only, split lengthwise, cut crosswise into thin slices, and washed well, or 12 scallions including green tops, sliced

1 teaspoon salt

½ cup canned low-sodium chicken broth or homemade stock

1 cup heavy cream

½ pound smoked turkey, sliced about ⅛-inch thick and cut into ¼-by-1½-inch strips

2 tablespoons chopped parsley

¼ teaspoon fresh-ground black pepper

¾ pound spaghetti

1. In a large frying pan, melt the butter over moderate heat. Add the leeks and salt and cook, stirring occasionally, until the leeks are tender, about 10 minutes.

2. Add the broth, increase the heat to moderately high, and simmer until the liquid is reduced to about ¼ cup. Stir in the cream and bring to a simmer. Reduce the heat and simmer until slightly thickened, 2 to 3 minutes. Stir in the turkey, parsley, and pepper.

3. In a large pot of boiling, salted water, cook the spaghetti until just done, about 12 minutes. Drain and toss with the sauce.

Meat

FETTUCCINE WITH FIVE-SPICE PORK AND CARROTS

Don't be tempted to cook the pork tenderloin any longer than specified, or you'll risk losing its juicy tenderness. By the time you combine it with the hot carrots and sauce and toss it with the pasta, it will be perfectly done.

WINE RECOMMENDATION
A dry but aromatic white wine will work nicely with the light pork as well as the assertive flavors of the fresh ginger and the Chinese spices. Try a dry riesling either from Alsace in France or from California.

SERVES 4

1   pound pork tenderloin

     Salt

     Fresh-ground black pepper

     Chinese five-spice powder

3   tablespoons cooking oil

4   carrots, cut in half lengthwise and then crosswise into ¼-inch slices

1   teaspoon sugar

4   scallions including green tops, chopped

4   cloves garlic, cut into thin slices

1   tablespoon chopped fresh ginger

1   jalapeño pepper, seeds and ribs removed, chopped

1   cup canned low-sodium chicken broth or homemade stock

2   tablespoons soy sauce

½   pound fettuccine or Chinese egg noodles

1. Cut the pork into ½-inch slices and flatten them with the heel of your hand. Sprinkle the pork with ⅛ teaspoon each salt and pepper and ¼ teaspoon five-spice powder. In a large frying pan, heat 1 tablespoon of the oil over moderate heat. Cook the pork, in two batches if necessary, until just done, about 1 minute per side. Remove the pork from the pan, let sit for 5 minutes, and then cut it into strips.

2. In the same pan, heat the remaining 2 tablespoons oil over moderate heat. Add the carrots and sugar and cook, stirring frequently, until starting to brown, about 3 minutes. Stir in the scallions, garlic, ginger, and jalapeño. Cook, stirring, for 2 minutes longer. Add the broth, soy sauce, ½ teaspoon salt, and ⅛ teaspoon five-spice powder and simmer until the sauce begins to thicken, about 4 minutes. Stir in the pork and any accumulated juice and remove the sauce from the heat.

3. In a large pot of boiling, salted water, cook the fettuccine until just done, about 12 minutes. Drain and toss with the sauce.

PASTA, TOFU, PORK, AND CHINESE CABBAGE IN GINGER BROTH

Serve this Asian pasta in a bowl with a spoon as well as a fork so that you can get all the flavorful broth. We use spaghettini here, but if you have dried Chinese egg noodles, by all means use them.

WINE RECOMMENDATION
With an assertive dish like this, the wine should have plenty of acidity and very little delicacy. A California sparkling wine or a Vouvray (made from chenin blanc grapes) would be best.

SERVES 4

- 3 cups canned low-sodium chicken broth or homemade stock
- 6 tablespoons soy sauce
- 1/4 cup rice-wine vinegar
- 1/4 cup mirin
- 1 tablespoon minced fresh ginger
- 2 cloves garlic, minced
- 2 teaspoons Asian sesame oil
- 2 teaspoons sugar
- 1 1/2 teaspoons salt
- 3/4 pound spaghettini
- 3/4 pound Chinese cabbage, cut into 2-inch pieces
- 1/2 pound firm tofu, cut into 3/4-inch cubes
- 1/3 pound pork loin chop, cut into 1/8-inch slices about 1/2 inch wide and 1 1/2 inches long
- 3 scallions including green tops, sliced

1. In a medium stainless-steel saucepan, combine the broth, soy sauce, vinegar, mirin, ginger, garlic, sesame oil, sugar, and salt. Bring just to a simmer, stirring occasionally.

2. In a large pot of boiling, salted water cook the spaghettini until almost done, about 8 minutes. Drain. Return the pasta to the pot.

3. Add the hot ginger broth to the pasta along with the cabbage and tofu. Bring back to a simmer and cook for 1 minute. Add the pork and scallions. Remove from the heat and let sit until the pork is just done, about 1 minute.

MIRIN SUBSTITUTE

In place of mirin, a sweet low-alcohol Japanese cooking wine, you can use 3 tablespoons sweet sherry, or 3 tablespoons dry sherry plus 1 1/2 tablespoons sugar.

ZITI WITH PORK AND ESCAROLE IN CREAMY THYME SAUCE

Quick-cooking pork tenderloin stars here with a strong back-up from just-wilted ribbons of escarole, and a touch of mustard to complement both.

A dry riesling from the Alsace region in France makes a perfect partner for pork and stands up well to the mustard here.

SERVES 4

- 1 pound pork tenderloin
- ¾ teaspoon salt
- ½ teaspoon fresh-ground black pepper
- 3 tablespoons cooking oil
- ½ pound escarole, leaves cut crosswise into ½-inch strips (about 4 cups)
- 1 shallot or 2 scallions including green tops, chopped
- ½ cup canned low-sodium chicken broth or homemade stock
- ½ teaspoon dried thyme
- 2 teaspoons grainy or Dijon mustard
- ½ cup heavy cream
- ½ pound ziti

1. Cut the pork into ½-inch slices and flatten them with the heel of your hand. Sprinkle the pork with ¼ teaspoon each of the salt and pepper. In a large frying pan, heat 2 tablespoons of the oil over moderate heat. Cook the pork, in two batches if necessary, until just barely done, about 1 minute per side. Remove the pork from the pan, let it sit for 5 minutes, and then cut into thin strips.

2. In the same pan, heat the remaining 1 tablespoon of the oil over moderate heat. Add the escarole, shallot, ¼ teaspoon of the salt, and the remaining ¼ teaspoon pepper and cook, stirring until the escarole wilts, about 1 minute. Add the broth and the thyme and simmer until the broth is reduced to ¼ cup, about 3 minutes. Whisk in the mustard, cream, and the remaining ¼ teaspoon salt; bring just to a simmer. Add the pork and any accumulated juices to the sauce, and remove from the heat.

3. In a large pot of boiling, salted water, cook the ziti until just done, about 13 minutes. Drain and toss with the sauce.

WHOLE-WHEAT SPAGHETTI WITH SAUSAGE AND PEPPERS

Use mild or hot Italian sausage, according to your preference, in this updated classic. We call for red bell peppers but you can use green or one of each color. Plain spaghetti can replace the whole-wheat, too.

WINE RECOMMENDATION
The earthy Italian feel of this dish and the acidity from the tomatoes make a nebbiolo-based wine from the Piedmont region of Italy a nice choice. Look for a lighter version such as Nebbiolo d'Alba.

SERVES 4

- 1 tablespoon olive oil
- 1 pound mild or hot Italian sausage
- 1 onion, chopped
- 2 red bell peppers, cut into 1-inch pieces
- 1¾ teaspoons salt
- 3 cloves garlic, minced
- 1 cup canned crushed tomatoes in thick puree
- 1 cup canned low-sodium chicken broth or homemade stock
- 2 tablespoons dry vermouth or dry white wine
- 3 tablespoons chopped flat-leaf parsley
- ¾ pound whole-wheat spaghetti
- 2 tablespoons grated Parmesan cheese, plus more for serving

1. In a large frying pan, heat the oil over moderate heat. Add the sausage and cook, turning, until browned and cooked through, about 8 minutes. Remove. When the sausage is cool enough to handle, cut it into ½-inch slices.

2. Add the onion, peppers, and ¾ teaspoon of the salt to the pan. Cook, stirring frequently, until the vegetables begin to brown, about 5 minutes. Cover and cook, stirring occasionally until the vegetables are soft, about 3 minutes longer. Add the garlic and cook, stirring, for about 30 seconds. Add the tomatoes, broth, vermouth, the reserved sausage and any accumulated juices, the parsley, and the remaining 1 teaspoon salt and bring to a simmer.

3. In a large pot of boiling, salted water, cook the spaghetti until just done, about 12 minutes. Drain and toss with the sausage-and-pepper mixture and the Parmesan. Serve with additional Parmesan.

ACADIAN RIGATONI

Three ingredients form the foundation of Creole and Acadian cookery—onion, celery, and green bell pepper. Our dish starts with this trio and is enhanced by garlic, tomatoes, and the deliciously hot *andouille* sausage.

WINE RECOMMENDATION
The fiery sausage and the acidity of the tomatoes and peppers will go very well with a refreshing, slightly chilled red wine—a Chianti from Italy or a pinot noir from California.

SERVES 4

- 1   tablespoon cooking oil
- 1   pound *andouille* or other spicy sausage such as hot Italian, casings removed, sausage cut into 1-inch pieces
- 1   onion, chopped
- 2   ribs celery, chopped
- 1   large green bell pepper, chopped
- 2   cloves garlic, chopped
- 1½   cups canned crushed tomatoes in thick puree (one 16-ounce can)
- 1¼   teaspoons salt
- ½   teaspoon fresh-ground black pepper
- ¾   pound rigatoni

1. In a large frying pan, heat the oil over moderate heat. Add the sausage and cook, stirring, for 3 minutes. Stir in the onion, celery, green pepper, and garlic. Cover the pan and cook over moderately low heat, stirring occasionally, until the vegetables are soft, about 10 minutes. Add the tomatoes, salt, and black pepper. Cover and simmer for 15 minutes longer.

2. In a large pot of boiling, salted water, cook the rigatoni until just done, about 14 minutes. Drain and toss the pasta with the sauce.

VARIATION

CREAMY ACADIAN RIGATONI

For a creamy version of this dish, use 1½ tablespoons tomato paste, 1 cup of cream, and an additional ½ teaspoon of salt in place of the canned tomatoes in puree. This variation, while more luxurious, is actually a little quicker.

ANDOUILLE SUBSTITUTIONS

If neither *andouille* nor hot Italian sausage is available, use a mild sausage and add ¼ teaspoon of dried red-pepper flakes with the tomatoes and salt.

CAVATAPPI WITH CHORIZO AND BLACK BEANS

The full, earthy Tex-Mex flavors of chorizo, black beans, and chili blend perfectly, if somewhat unexpectedly, with corkscrew-shaped macaroni.

■ WINE RECOMMENDATION
A sparkling wine or crisp sauvignon blanc from California—or even a Mexican beer—is a good foil for this spicy dish.

SERVES 4

3 tablespoons cooking oil

1 onion, sliced thin

2 cloves garlic, chopped

½ teaspoon dried oregano

¾ teaspoon chili powder

½ pound cured chorizo or other spicy hard sausage such as pepperoni, casings removed and sausage cut into thin slices

1 tablespoon tomato paste

1 cup canned low-sodium chicken broth or homemade stock

1 cup canned black beans, drained and rinsed

1 tablespoon lime juice

1 teaspoon salt

½ pound cavatappi

⅓ cup chopped fresh parsley

1. In a large frying pan, heat the oil over moderately low heat. Add the onion and sauté until it begins to soften, about 3 minutes. Stir in the garlic, oregano, and chili powder and cook, stirring, for 2 minutes.

2. Add the chorizo, tomato paste, and broth to the pan and stir. Bring to a simmer and cook, stirring occasionally, until slightly thickened, about 3 minutes. Add the black beans, the lime juice, and the salt and remove the pan from the heat.

3. In a large pot of boiling, salted water, cook the cavatappi until just done, about 13 minutes. Drain; toss with the sauce and parsley.

TEST-KITCHEN TIPS

■ For firm canned black beans rather than the usual mushy, overprocessed specimens, we prefer the Goya brand.

■ If you use tomato paste in small quantities, consider buying a tube of one of the imported Italian brands. The tube lasts a long time in the refrigerator, just like anchovy paste, so you won't have to open a whole can for one or two tablespoons.

MACARONI WITH SUMMER SQUASH, SALAMI, AND RICOTTA TOMATO SAUCE

Sun-dried tomatoes add lots of flavor to the sauce. If you prefer zucchini, you can use it in place of the summer squash.

WINE RECOMMENDATION
We suggest you look for a refreshing white wine to pair with this lively, Italian-inspired dish. A pinot grigio or a Galestro from Italy will serve admirably.

SERVES 4

2 tablespoons cooking oil

1½ pounds summer squash (about 4), grated

3 cloves garlic, minced

¾ teaspoon salt

1 teaspoon dried oregano

½ cup ricotta cheese

½ cup sun-dried tomatoes packed in oil, drained and chopped

¼ pound sliced salami, cut into thin strips

⅛ teaspoon fresh-ground black pepper

¾ pound elbow macaroni

¼ cup grated Parmesan cheese

1. In a large frying pan, heat the oil over moderately high heat. Add the summer squash, minced garlic, salt, and the oregano and cook, stirring, until tender, about 5 minutes. Add the ricotta cheese, sun-dried tomatoes, salami, and the pepper.

2. In a large pot of boiling, salted water, cook the macaroni until just done, about 8 minutes. Drain and toss the pasta with the sauce. Top with the Parmesan.

SUN-DRIED TOMATOES

Oil-packed sun-dried tomatoes come in a jar and need only to be drained before using. Sun-dried tomatoes are also available without the oil, usually in cellophane bags (for instructions on reconstituting the tomatoes, see page 47). You can substitute one type for the other.

FETTUCCINE WITH GOAT-CHEESE AND SALAMI SAUCE

Goat cheese and salami? Yes, the two taste wonderful together—and on pasta.

WINE RECOMMENDATION
A sauvignon blanc goes well with goat cheese. Either a Pouilly-Fumé from the Loire Valley in France or a California sauvignon blanc is a good choice.

SERVES 4

¾ pound fettuccine

1 tablespoon butter

3 cloves garlic, minced

¾ cup canned low-sodium chicken broth or homemade stock

½ cup heavy cream

¼ pound mild goat cheese, such as Montrachet

¼ pound salami, cut into ¼-inch cubes

3 tablespoons chopped fresh basil or parsley

¼ teaspoon fresh-ground black pepper

1. In a large pot of boiling, salted water, cook the fettuccine until just done, about 12 minutes.

2. Meanwhile, in a large pot, melt the butter over low heat. Add the garlic and cook, stirring, until soft, 3 to 5 minutes. Raise the heat to moderately low. Add the broth; bring to a simmer. Stir in the cream and bring just back to a simmer. Add the goat cheese and whisk until smooth. Stir in the salami, basil, and the pepper.

3. Drain the fettuccine and add to the sauce. Heat, stirring, over very low heat for 1 to 2 minutes, to allow the pasta to absorb some of the sauce.

CAVATAPPI WITH PEPPERONI

Pepperoni gives this sauce its kick. Or try other hot sausages such as cured chorizo.

WINE RECOMMENDATION
Look for a gulpable, fruity merlot to go with this full-flavored dish. Try a version from California or experiment with a bottle from Chile or Argentina.

SERVES 4

4   ounces thin-sliced pepperoni, slices cut in half

2   tablespoons olive oil

1   large onion, chopped

1   red or green bell pepper, chopped

2   cloves garlic, minced

1½ cups canned tomatoes with their juice (one 16-ounce can)

¾   teaspoon salt

¾   pound cavatappi

3   tablespoons chopped flat-leaf parsley

1. In a large frying pan, sauté the pepperoni over moderate heat until lightly browned, about 3 minutes. Transfer to paper towels to drain. Pour off the fat from the pan and wipe the pan clean.

2. In the same pan, heat the oil over moderately low heat. Add the onion and pepper and cook, stirring occasionally, until soft, about 10 minutes. Add the garlic and cook, stirring, for 30 seconds. Stir in the tomatoes with their juice, breaking them up. Add the salt, cover, and simmer over low heat for 10 minutes.

3. In a large pot of boiling, salted water, cook the cavatappi until just done, about 13 minutes. Drain and toss with the sauce, the pepperoni, and the parsley.

VARIATION

CAVATAPPI WITH PEPPERONI AND ORANGE TOMATO SAUCE

For an additional Mediterranean touch, stir the grated zest of 1 orange into the tomato sauce just before you remove it from the heat.

SPAGHETTI WITH CREAMY CORN AND HAM

Here's a great way to celebrate the abundance of summer corn. If you can't get good fresh corn, though, use three cups of frozen kernels, thawed, and put them directly into the food processor with the cream. Since frozen corn is parboiled, the heat of the pasta is enough to finish cooking it.

WINE RECOMMENDATION
For this all-American dish, you might want to try an American white wine from a lesser known, East Coast region. Look for a fairly acidic chardonnay or sauvignon blanc from Virginia, the Finger Lakes region of New York, or even Rhode Island.

SERVES 4

4   large ears corn, husks and silk removed

¾   cup heavy cream

3   tablespoons chopped flat-leaf parsley

½   teaspoon salt

¼   teaspoon fresh-ground black pepper

¾   pound spaghetti

¼   pound sliced, smoked ham, cut into thin strips

2   tablespoons butter, cut into pieces

1. In a large pot of boiling, salted water, cook the ears of corn until just done, about 3 minutes. Remove the corn from the pot and save the hot water to cook the spaghetti. When the ears of corn are cool enough to handle, cut the kernels off the cob. You should have about 3 cups of kernels.

2. Put the corn in a food processor with the cream, parsley, salt, and pepper. Pulse three or four times to chop the corn to a coarse puree.

3. Return the water to a boil. Add the spaghetti and cook until just done, about 12 minutes. Reserve about ¾ cup of the pasta water. Drain the spaghetti and toss with ⅓ cup of the reserved pasta water, the corn mixture, the ham, and the butter. If the sauce seems too thick, add more of the reserved pasta water.

TEST-KITCHEN TIP

To cut the kernels from an ear of corn, break the ear in half with your hands, or cut it with a knife. Stand each half on end on a cutting board and, using a large knife, cut straight down the sides to remove the kernels. It's easier to cut the kernels off cooked corn than raw because the juice splatters less.

Bow Ties with Sweet Potatoes and Canadian Bacon

Bow-tie pasta with slices of sweet potato, diced Canadian bacon, and tomato puree form a harmonious dish of varied flavors, shapes, and colors. We use sage here, but if you don't care for it, try the same quantity of thyme instead.

WINE RECOMMENDATION
To match the sweetness of both the potato and the Canadian bacon, try a kabinett riesling from Germany's Mosel-Saar-Ruwer region.

SERVES 4

- 2 tablespoons cooking oil
- 1 onion, halved and cut into thin slices
- 1 sweet potato (about ½ pound), peeled, cut in half lengthwise, then cut crosswise into ¼-inch slices
- ¼ cup water
- 1 teaspoon dried sage
- ⅛ teaspoon cayenne
- ½ teaspoon salt
- 1½ cups canned crushed tomatoes in thick puree (one 16-ounce can)
- ½ pound Canadian bacon, diced
- ¾ pound bow ties

1. In a large frying pan, heat the oil over moderately low heat. Add the onion and sweet potato and toss to coat with the oil. Add the water, cover, and cook until the onions are soft, about 5 minutes. Stir in the sage, cayenne, salt, and tomatoes. Reduce the heat and simmer, covered, until the sweet potato is tender and the sauce thickened, about 15 minutes. Add the Canadian bacon and remove from the heat.

2. In a large pot of boiling, salted water, cook the bow ties until just done, about 15 minutes. Drain and toss the pasta with the sauce.

VARIATIONS

Bow Ties with Sweet Potatoes and Ham

Dice ½ pound of ham and use it in place of the Canadian bacon.

Bow Ties with Canadian Bacon and Squash

Peel and dice ½ pound of winter squash, such as butternut or Hubbard, and use it in place of the sweet potato. Depending on the type of squash, you may need to adjust the simmering time by a few minutes.

Bow-Tie Salad with Fennel, Prosciutto, and Parmesan

A tangy lemon dressing makes this main-course salad especially refreshing, and the only thing you have to cook is the pasta. If you find a fennel bulb with the dark-green feathery tops still on, chop some of them and toss into the pasta.

WINE RECOMMENDATION

Have some fun with this dish and try a bottle of the sparkling Italian wine Prosecco. It should go nicely with the fennel.

SERVES 4

½ pound bow ties

1 large fennel bulb (about 1 pound), sliced as thin as possible

¼ cup olive oil

2 tablespoons lemon juice

¼ teaspoon salt

½ teaspoon fresh-ground black pepper

¼ pound thin-sliced prosciutto, cut into strips

¼-pound chunk Parmesan cheese, or ⅓ cup grated Parmesan

1. In a large pot of boiling, salted water, cook the bow ties until just done, about 15 minutes. Drain. Rinse with cold water and drain thoroughly.

2. In a large bowl, toss together the bow ties, fennel, oil, lemon juice, salt, and ¼ teaspoon of the pepper. Add the prosciutto and toss again.

3. To serve, mound the salad on plates. Top with strips of Parmesan shaved from the chunk of cheese with a vegetable peeler or with the grated Parmesan. Sprinkle the remaining ¼ teaspoon pepper over the cheese.

Test-Kitchen Tip

The easiest way to slice fennel is to cut off the stalks, cut the bulb in half from the top through the root end, lay each half flat-side down, and slice. For that matter, this is a good technique for almost any round fruit or vegetable.

ORECCHIETTE WITH PROSCIUTTO AND MELON

Don't be afraid of this strange-sounding dish. The prosciutto-and-melon combination we've always loved as an hors d'oeuvre tastes great with pasta and tomato sauce, too.

WINE RECOMMENDATION
A fairly acidic white with a hint of mellowness and fruit is a good match for this unique dish. Try a pinot blanc from the Alsace region of France or a non-oaky California chardonnay.

SERVES 4

2	tablespoons butter
1	onion, chopped
¼	pound sliced prosciutto, cut into thin strips
1½	cups canned crushed tomatoes in thick puree (one 16-ounce can)
1	cup diced cantaloupe (from about ½ melon)
½	cup light cream or half-and-half
1	teaspoon salt
¾	teaspoon fresh-ground black pepper
¾	pound orecchiette

1. In a large frying pan, melt the butter over moderately low heat. Add the onion and cook, stirring occasionally, until translucent, about 5 minutes. Add the prosciutto and tomatoes. Cover, reduce the heat, and simmer for 10 minutes. Add the cantaloupe, cream, and the salt and pepper. Cook until heated through, about 3 minutes longer.

2. In a large pot of boiling, salted water, cook the orecchiette until done, about 15 minutes. Drain the pasta and toss it with the sauce.

TIME-SAVING TIP

Purchase precut cantaloupe from the salad bar at your grocery store to save fiddling with a whole melon.

LINGUINE WITH BROCCOLI RABE, PANCETTA, AND PINE NUTS

The classic combination of broccoli rabe, garlic, and a touch of hot red pepper is enhanced here by pine nuts and strips of pancetta. If the pancetta is especially lean, you may need to add another tablespoon of olive oil. To substitute bacon for the pancetta, use the same quantity but increase the salt to a half teaspoon.

WINE RECOMMENDATION
A crisp white wine is the best idea for this dish as it will cut through the salt of the meat and the richness of the nuts. Choose a chenin-blanc-based wine from the Loire Valley in France such as a Savennières or Anjou. Make sure it is dry (not demi-sec).

SERVES 4

¼ cup pine nuts

¼ pound pancetta, cut into ½-inch pieces

3 tablespoons olive oil

4 cloves garlic, minced

¼ teaspoon dried red-pepper flakes

1 pound broccoli rabe, tough ends removed, cut into 1½-inch lengths

¼ teaspoon salt

¾ pound linguine

1. Heat the oven to 350°. Toast the pine nuts in the oven until they are golden brown, about 8 minutes.

2. In a large frying pan, cook the pancetta with the oil over moderate heat until beginning to crisp. Add the garlic and red-pepper flakes and cook, stirring, for 1 minute.

3. In a large pot of boiling, salted water, cook the broccoli rabe until almost done, about 3 minutes. Drain. Add the broccoli rabe to the frying pan along with the salt and cook, stirring, for 2 minutes.

4. In a large pot of boiling, salted water, cook the linguine until just done, about 12 minutes. Drain and toss with the broccoli rabe and pine nuts.

ROTELLE WITH BACON, WATERCRESS, AND CHERRY TOMATOES

Here watercress and cherry tomatoes cook for only a matter of minutes, just long enough to soften them slightly. The watercress adds a nice bite, but if you don't like that effect, try strips of romaine or another mild green.

WINE RECOMMENDATION
A straightforward white wine will be best. Either a pinot blanc from Alsace in France or a California chenin blanc will have enough body to stand up to the acidity of the tomatoes and the saltiness of the bacon in this dish.

SERVES 4

½ pound sliced bacon, cut crosswise into ½-inch strips

1½ cups cherry tomatoes, halved

1 teaspoon salt

¾ teaspoon fresh-ground black pepper

1 bunch watercress (about 5 ounces), tough stems removed

¾ pound rotelle

2 tablespoons butter

2 tablespoons olive oil

1 scallion including green top, cut into thin slices

Grated Parmesan cheese, for serving

1. In a large frying pan, cook the bacon until golden brown and just crisp, about 5 minutes. Remove with a slotted spoon and drain on paper towels. Pour off all but 1 teaspoon of the fat.

2. Add the tomatoes, salt, and pepper to the pan. Cook over moderate heat, stirring, until the tomatoes soften slightly, about 3 minutes. Add the watercress and cook, stirring, until just wilted, about 1 minute.

3. In a large pot of boiling, salted water, cook the rotelle until just done, about 12 minutes. Reserve ¾ cup of the pasta water. Drain the pasta and toss with the bacon, ½ cup of the reserved pasta water, the tomato mixture, the butter, and the olive oil. If the pasta seems dry, add more of the reserved pasta water. Top with the sliced scallions. Serve with grated Parmesan.

LINGUINE CARBONARA

No book about quick pastas would be complete without a version of this classic. It's made with little more than bacon and eggs.

WINE RECOMMENDATION
An uncomplicated, fairly acidic and non-oaky white wine will cut through the richness of the bacon, eggs, and cheese in this dish. Either a vernaccia or a pinot bianco from Italy fits the bill.

SERVES 4

- 2 tablespoons olive oil
- 2 tablespoons butter
- ¼ pound sliced bacon, cut crosswise into thin strips
- 2 cloves garlic, minced
- ½ cup red wine
- ½ teaspoon fresh-ground black pepper
- 2 eggs
- ½ cup grated Parmesan cheese, plus more for serving
- ½ teaspoon salt
- ¾ pound linguine
- 2 tablespoons chopped fresh parsley

1. In a small stainless-steel frying pan, heat the oil and butter over moderate heat. Add the bacon and cook until brown but not crisp, about 4 minutes. Add the garlic, wine, and pepper. Simmer until the wine is reduced to 2 tablespoons, about 3 minutes. Remove from the heat. In a large bowl, whisk together the eggs, cheese, and salt.

2. In a large pot of boiling, salted water, cook the linguine until just done, about 12 minutes. Drain the pasta, add it to the egg-and-cheese mixture, and toss quickly. Pour the bacon mixture over the linguine. Add the parsley and toss just until mixed. Serve immediately with additional Parmesan.

VARIATION

CLASSIC LINGUINE CARBONARA

This carbonara would be equally delicious (and more authentic) using the same quantity of pancetta in place of the bacon. You can also substitute white wine for the red if you prefer.

LINGUINE WITH ONION, BACON, AND PARMESAN

The browned onions lend a slight sweetness to this dish. If you prefer not to have that caramelized flavor, just soften the onions for five minutes without browning them, or try the variation below using leeks.

WINE RECOMMENDATION
Though the dish is Italian, the ingredients make one think of an Alsatian quiche. A riesling from this French region will work beautifully with this pasta.

SERVES 4

½ pound sliced bacon, cut crosswise into ½-inch strips

2 onions, sliced thin

½ teaspoon dried thyme

⅛ teaspoon dried red-pepper flakes

1 teaspoon salt

¾ pound linguine

½ cup grated Parmesan cheese, plus more for serving

2 tablespoons chopped fresh parsley

½ teaspoon fresh-ground black pepper

1. In a large frying pan, cook the bacon until crisp. Remove the bacon with a slotted spoon and drain on paper towels. Pour off all but 2 tablespoons of the bacon fat. Put the pan over moderate heat. Add the onions, the thyme, the red-pepper flakes, and ¼ teaspoon of the salt. Cook, stirring occasionally, until the onions are brown, about 10 minutes. Remove from the heat.

2. In a large pot of boiling, salted water, cook the linguine until just done, about 12 minutes. Reserve 1 cup of the pasta water. Drain the linguine and toss with the bacon, onions, ¾ cup of the reserved pasta water, the Parmesan, parsley, the remaining ¾ teaspoon salt, and the pepper. If the sauce seems too thick, add more of the pasta water. Serve with additional Parmesan cheese.

VARIATION

LINGUINE WITH LEEKS, PANCETTA, AND PARMESAN

Substitute ½ pound of pancetta for the bacon, and 1½ cups of sliced leeks, white and light-green parts only (from about 3 medium leeks), for the onion.

PERCIATELLI WITH MEAT SAUCE AND FONTINA

Remember the meat sauce that Mom used to cook all day long? This version tastes as good, but can be made in only fifteen minutes. Perciatelli and bucatini are interchangeable; spaghetti would be fine here, too.

WINE RECOMMENDATION
The meatiness of this dish and the acidity of the tomatoes make a Sangiovese-grape-based wine ideal. Look for a Chianti Classico or a Rosso de Montalcino from the Tuscan region of Italy.

SERVES 4

  1 tablespoon cooking oil

  1 onion, chopped

  1 pound ground beef

  ½ cup red wine

1½ cups canned crushed tomatoes in thick puree (one 16-ounce can)

  1 teaspoon dried oregano

2¼ teaspoons salt

  ¾ teaspoon fresh-ground black pepper

  ½ pound perciatelli

  ½ teaspoon red-wine vinegar

  2 ounces Fontina cheese, grated

  ⅓ cup grated Parmesan cheese, plus more for serving

  ¼ cup chopped fresh parsley

1. In a large stainless-steel frying pan, heat the oil over moderate heat. Add the onion and cook until starting to soften, about 3 minutes. Add the ground beef and cook until the meat is no longer pink, about 2 minutes. Stir in the wine and simmer until reduced to ¼ cup, about 2 minutes. Add the tomatoes, oregano, and the salt and pepper. Reduce the heat, cover, and simmer for 15 minutes.

2. In a large pot of boiling, salted water, cook the perciatelli until just done, about 15 minutes. Drain and toss with the meat sauce, vinegar, Fontina, Parmesan, and parsley. Serve with additional Parmesan.

PASTA BOLOGNESE

We find this sauce, which is traditionally simmered for a long time, tastes just as good when cooked for less than half an hour. Now you won't have to consign Bolognese sauce to the lazy Sunday afternoon of cooking that never comes.

WINE RECOMMENDATION
Chianti pairs well with this classic sauce. A zinfandel from California would be an American alternative.

SERVES 4

2 tablespoons butter

¼ pound sliced bacon, cut crosswise into ¼-inch strips

1 onion, chopped

½ pound ground beef or a mixture of pork, veal, and beef (meat-loaf mix)

1 cup canned low-sodium beef or chicken broth or homemade stock

½ cup dry white wine

2 tablespoons tomato paste

½ teaspoon dried oregano

¾ teaspoon salt

¼ teaspoon fresh-ground black pepper

½ cup heavy cream

¾ pound spaghetti

2 tablespoons chopped fresh parsley

1. In a large frying pan, heat the butter and bacon over moderately low heat. Cook until the bacon renders some of its fat, about 3 minutes. Add the onion and cook, stirring occasionally, until starting to soften, about 3 minutes longer.

Stir in the ground beef and cook until the meat is no longer pink, about 2 minutes. Add the broth, wine, tomato paste, oregano, salt, and pepper. Simmer, stirring occasionally, until the sauce thickens, about 25 minutes. Stir in the cream and remove from the heat.

2. In a large pot of boiling, salted water, cook the spaghetti until just done, about 12 minutes. Drain and toss with the sauce and the parsley.

TEX-MEX CAVATAPPI

Flavors of the Southwest—cilantro, lime, chili, and salsa—come together here on corkscrew-shaped macaroni. Chunky salsa works as a great ready-made sauce for pasta.

WINE RECOMMENDATION
The spiciness of the salsa and chili powder combined with the acidity of the lime make a very high-acid white wine an obvious choice. We favor a sauvignon blanc from California.

SERVES 4

 2 tablespoons cooking oil

 1 pound ground beef

1½ teaspoons chili powder

1½ teaspoons salt

 ¼ teaspoon fresh-ground black pepper

 2 cups (one 16-ounce jar) chunky tomato salsa

 ¾ pound cavatappi

 2 teaspoons lime juice or red-wine vinegar

 ¼ cup chopped cilantro or parsley

 6 ounces cheddar cheese, grated (about 1½ cups)

 Lime wedges for serving (optional)

1. In a large frying pan, heat the oil over moderately high heat. Add the ground beef and cook until browned, about 3 minutes. Stir in the chili powder, salt, and pepper. Add the salsa and simmer over low heat to allow the flavors to combine, about 10 minutes.

2. In a large pot of boiling, salted water, cook the cavatappi until just done, about 13 minutes. Drain the pasta and toss it with the sauce, lime juice, cilantro, and 1 cup of the cheese. Stir until the cheese is melted. Sprinkle with the remaining ½ cup cheese and serve with wedges of lime if you like.

SALSA SELECTION

There are several brands of salsa on the market today. Choose according to your taste (mild, medium, or hot) and pick one of high quality; the finished dish will only be as good as your salsa. A smoked-chile variety would be a delicious possibility to try.

TORTELLINI WITH GARLIC SAGE BUTTER SAUCE

Leaves of fresh sage sautéed in golden-brown butter form a classic Italian pasta sauce (see last Variation below). Our version uses ground sage, and so you can make it any time of the year. We've added a generous amount of garlic, too. Slowly cooking it in the butter mellows its pungency, but you can also use fewer cloves if you prefer.

WINE RECOMMENDATION
Barbera is one of the most food-friendly Italian red wines, and it works beautifully here with the assertive sage and garlic.

SERVES 4

6	tablespoons butter
6	cloves garlic, smashed
½	teaspoon ground sage
1	teaspoon salt
⅛	teaspoon fresh-ground black pepper
1	pound fresh or frozen meat-filled tortellini
2	tablespoons chopped flat-leaf parsley

1. In a medium frying pan, melt the butter over low heat. Add the garlic and cook, stirring occasionally and mashing the garlic with the back of a wooden spoon, until it is soft and golden, 10 to 12 minutes. Stir in the sage, salt, and pepper.

2. In a large pot of boiling, salted water, cook the tortellini until just done, about 4 minutes for fresh and 12 minutes for frozen. Drain the pasta and return to the pot.

3. Add the butter and parsley and toss over low heat until the pasta is thoroughly coated with the butter, about 1 minute.

VARIATIONS

RAVIOLI WITH GARLIC SAGE BUTTER SAUCE

Feel free to use ravioli, or any other small stuffed pasta, instead of the tortellini.

CHEESE TORTELLINI WITH GARLIC SAGE BUTTER SAUCE

If you prefer another stuffing, such as cheese or mushroom, by all means try it.

TORTELLINI WITH GARLIC AND FRESH-SAGE BUTTER SAUCE

Substitute 1 tablespoon of chopped fresh sage for the dried. Sauté until crisp but not brown, about 1 minute.

PENNE SALAD WITH ROAST BEEF, ARUGULA, RADICCHIO, AND CAPERS

Sliced rare roast beef from the deli counter turns pasta salad into dinner. Sweet balsamic vinegar balances the slightly bitter greens, and shavings of Parmesan cheese on top are a deliciously stylish garnish.

WINE RECOMMENDATION
This salad goes well with many simple, fruity reds. Pour a Beaujolais-Villages or try a red wine from the south of France such as Corbières or Coteaux du Languedoc.

SERVES 4

¾ pound penne

¼ pound arugula (about 2 bunches), stems removed, leaves torn into pieces

1 head radicchio (about 6 ounces), torn into pieces

¼ cup drained capers

6 tablespoons olive oil

3½ tablespoons balsamic vinegar

¾ teaspoon salt

½ teaspoon fresh-ground black pepper

½ pound thin-sliced cooked roast beef, cut into strips

2-ounce chunk Parmesan cheese, or 3 tablespoons grated Parmesan

1. In a large pot of boiling, salted water, cook the penne until just done, about 13 minutes. Drain, rinse with cold water, and drain thoroughly.

2. In a large bowl, toss the pasta with the arugula, radicchio, capers, oil, vinegar, salt, and ¼ teaspoon of the pepper. Add the roast beef and toss again.

3. To serve, mound the salad on plates. Top each with strips of Parmesan shaved from the chunk of cheese with a vegetable peeler or with the grated Parmesan. Sprinkle the remaining ¼ teaspoon pepper over the salads.

PENNE WITH CHILI-RUBBED FLANK STEAK AND PINEAPPLE SALSA

The sweet, the savory, and the spicy join in this unusual and delicious dish. To be tender, flank steak needs to cook either fast and hot or long and slow. Here the method is a brief broil.

WINE RECOMMENDATION
The combination of flavors in this dish welcomes an exuberantly fruity bottle of merlot with soft tannins. Experiment with one from a California producer.

SERVES 4

- 1 pound flank steak
- ¼ cup plus 1 teaspoon cooking oil
- ¾ teaspoon chili powder
- ¾ teaspoon salt
- ½ cup crushed pineapple, drained (from an 8-ounce can)
- ½ jalapeño pepper with seeds, chopped
- 1 small red onion, chopped
- 1 tablespoon lime juice
- ¼ cup chopped cilantro or parsley
- ¼ teaspoon fresh-ground black pepper
- ½ pound penne

1. Heat the broiler. Rub the flank steak with the 1 teaspoon oil, ½ teaspoon of the chili powder, and ¼ teaspoon of the salt. Broil the meat until medium rare, about 4 minutes per side. Let it rest for 5 minutes and then cut it diagonally into slices.

2. In a large glass or stainless-steel bowl, combine the pineapple, the remaining ¼ cup oil, the jalapeño pepper, onion, lime juice, cilantro, black pepper, and the remaining ½ teaspoon salt and ¼ teaspoon chili powder. Stir in the sliced steak.

3. In a large pot of boiling, salted water, cook the penne until just done, about 13 minutes. Drain and toss with the salsa and steak.

RIGATONI WITH SIRLOIN AND GORGONZOLA SAUCE

This full-flavored dish will satisfy the heartiest of appetites. Roquefort cheese would also taste terrific in the sauce.

WINE RECOMMENDATION
Gorgonzola is salty, sharp, and assertive, which makes it tough to pair with wine. Your best bet is a straightforward red with fine acidity, such as a barbera from the Piedmont region of Italy or a Beaujolais-Villages from France.

SERVES 4

- 2 tablespoons cooking oil
- 1 pound sirloin steak, cut into 1-inch cubes
- 1½ teaspoons salt
- ¾ teaspoon fresh-ground black pepper
- ½ pound portobello mushrooms, stems removed, caps cut in half and then sliced crosswise
- 1 shallot or 2 scallions including green tops, minced
- ¾ cup canned low-sodium chicken broth or homemade stock
- ¼ teaspoon Worcestershire sauce
- 3 ounces Gorgonzola or other blue cheese
- ½ cup heavy cream
- 2 tablespoons chopped fresh parsley
- ¾ pound rigatoni

1. In a large frying pan, heat 1 tablespoon of the oil over moderate heat. Season the steak with ¼ teaspoon each of the salt and pepper and add it to the pan. Brown on all sides, about 4 minutes, and remove. The meat should be medium rare.

2. Add the remaining 1 tablespoon oil to the hot pan, along with the mushrooms and ¼ teaspoon of the salt. Cook for about 2 minutes. Remove the mushrooms from the pan and add to the steak.

3. Add the shallot, broth, and Worcestershire sauce to the hot pan. Cook, stirring, to dislodge any browned bits that cling to the bottom of the pan. Simmer until the liquid is reduced to about ⅓ cup, approximately 5 minutes.

4. Add the cheese and the cream to the pan along with the steak and mushrooms and any accumulated juices, the remaining 1 teaspoon salt and ½ teaspoon pepper, and the parsley. Simmer to heat through, about 1 minute.

5. Meanwhile, in a large pot of boiling, salted water, cook the rigatoni until just done, about 14 minutes. Drain the pasta and toss it with the sauce.

FETTUCCINE WITH VEAL, PEAS, AND MINT

With the veal scaloppine, peas, and mint, this pasta is springlike, although you can make it year-round. Buy frozen petit peas, which are as good as—if not better than—what's usually available fresh and are a lot easier to prepare.

WINE RECOMMENDATION

A light and acidic vinho verde from Portugal or a sauvignon blanc from the Loire Valley in France, such as Pouilly-Fumé, will mirror the refreshing flavor of the mint.

SERVES 4

- 2 tablespoons butter
- 2 tablespoons olive oil
- ½ pound veal scaloppine, cut into 1-by-2-inch strips
- 1 teaspoon salt
- 1 small onion, chopped fine
- 2 tablespoons dry vermouth or dry white wine
- 1 cup canned low-sodium chicken broth or homemade stock
- 1 cup heavy cream
- 1 cup frozen petit peas
- ¾ pound fettuccine
- ¼ teaspoon fresh-ground black pepper
- ⅓ cup lightly packed mint leaves, cut into thin strips

1. In a large frying pan, melt 1 tablespoon of the butter with 1 tablespoon of the oil over moderately high heat. Add the veal and ¼ teaspoon salt and cook, turning, until just done, about 1 minute in all. Remove.

2. Reduce the heat to moderately low. Add the remaining 1 tablespoon oil and the onion. Cook, stirring occasionally, until translucent, about 5 minutes. Stir in the vermouth and then the broth and cream; bring to a simmer. Cook, stirring occasionally, until thickened, about 4 minutes. Add the peas and heat through, about 1 minute. Add the meat with any accumulated juices and the remaining ¾ teaspoon salt.

3. In a large pot of boiling, salted water, cook the fettuccine until just done, about 12 minutes. Drain. Toss with the sauce, the pepper, the remaining 1 tablespoon butter, and the mint. Let sit for 2 to 3 minutes so that the pasta absorbs some of the sauce.

FRESH MINT FLAVOR

Mint begins to lose flavor as soon as it's picked. Even if the bunch you're using looks fine, it may have been picked long enough ago so that the flavor is weak. Taste the sauce and, if you like, add more mint.

WHOLE-WHEAT SPAGHETTI WITH LAMB, TOMATO, AND CUMIN SAUCE

A Middle Eastern version of the spaghetti with meat sauce we all know and love, this pasta should find a ready audience. It's good with macaroni or with plain spaghetti.

WINE RECOMMENDATION

The spiciness of the cumin, the earthiness of the whole-wheat spaghetti, and the gaminess of the lamb are best with a full-bodied, slightly rough red wine such as a Côtes-du-Rhône from the southern part of France.

SERVES 4

2 tablespoons cooking oil

1 onion, chopped

2 cloves garlic, chopped

1 pound ground lamb

1 tablespoon ground cumin

1½ cups canned crushed tomatoes in thick puree (one 16-ounce can)

1¾ teaspoons salt

¾ pound whole-wheat spaghetti

½ teaspoon fresh-ground black pepper

⅓ cup chopped fresh mint or parsley

1. In a large frying pan, heat the oil over moderately low heat. Add the onion and cook, stirring occasionally, until translucent, about 5 minutes. Add the garlic and then the lamb. Cook until the meat is no longer pink, about 3 minutes. Stir in the cumin, tomatoes, and salt. Cover and simmer for 15 minutes.

2. In a large pot of boiling, salted water, cook the spaghetti until just done, about 15 minutes. Drain the pasta and toss it with the sauce, pepper, and mint.

VARIATION

WHOLE-WHEAT SPAGHETTI WITH MEAT SAUCE

You can substitute 1 pound of ground beef for the ground lamb. Use the same procedure, but decrease the cumin to 1½ teaspoons and use parsley rather than mint.

172

Planning Your Quick Meals

Look to this section for practical help in deciding what ingredients to keep on hand, what dish to make, and what simple wine to serve with it. Among the useful guides, you'll find a list of recipes in which you can include leftovers, for those times when you can't think what to do with the remainders of a roast chicken or the last of the boiled shrimp from a party, and ideas for seasonal and vegetarian pastas.

RECIPES PICTURED OPPOSITE: *(top)* pages 23, 129, 71; *(center)* pages 149, 123, 131; *(bottom)* pages 111, 143, 125

THE QUICK PANTRY

If you keep basic staples on hand, you can cut shopping to a minimum. Then you'll only have to make one short stop to pick up the fresh vegetables and meat you need to complete the recipe.

CUPBOARD

- anchovies
- apricots, dried
- artichoke hearts, canned
- beans, canned: black, chickpeas
- bread crumbs
- chicken broth, low-sodium
- clam juice
- coconut milk, unsweetened
- currants
- garlic
- honey
- oil: cooking, olive
- onions
- peanut butter
- peppers, roasted red
- pineapple, canned
- raisins
- soy sauce
- Tabasco sauce
- tomatoes: canned, paste, sun-dried
- tuna, packed in oil
- vinegar: balsamic, red- or white-wine, rice-wine
- Worcestershire sauce

LIQUOR CABINET

- Marsala
- port
- vermouth, dry white
- wine: dry white, red

SPICE SHELF

- bay leaves
- cayenne
- chili powder
- cinnamon
- coriander
- cumin
- curry powder
- fennel seeds
- five-spice powder
- ginger
- nutmeg
- oregano
- paprika
- red-pepper flakes
- rosemary
- sage
- tarragon
- thyme

FREEZER

- bacon
- frozen vegetables: Brussels sprouts, corn, peas
- nuts: pecans, pine nuts, walnuts
- stuffed pasta

REFRIGERATOR

- anchovy paste
- butter
- capers
- cheese: cheddar, Parmesan
- cream
- eggs
- fresh ginger
- jalapeño peppers
- lemons
- limes
- mustard: Dijon or grainy
- olives: black, green
- oranges
- parsley
- pesto
- salsa
- scallions
- sesame oil, Asian

Many recipes can be made with pantry items alone:

- Fettuccine Alfredo, *page 21 (variation)*
- Fettuccine Alfredo with Parsley and Sage, *page 21 (variation)*
- Fusilli with Artichoke Hearts and Parmesan Cream, *page 25*
- Spaghettini with Garlic and Oil, *page 33 (variation)*
- Spaghettini with Walnuts, Garlic, and Oil, *page 33 (variation)*
- Bow Ties with Sun-Dried Tomato and Scallion Cream, *page 47*
- Macaroni and Cheese, *page 61*
- Cheese Tortellini with Walnut Pesto, *page 67*
- Linguine with Gremolada, *page 71*
- Vermicelli Fra Diavolo, *page 77 (variation)*
- Fedelini with Tuna and Chickpeas, *page 95*
- Linguine Carbonara, *page 151*
- Linguine with Onion, Bacon, and Parmesan, *page 153*
- Tortellini with Garlic Sage Butter Sauce, *page 161*

SEASONAL PASTAS

So many vegetables and herbs are now available throughout the year that you can make most of our recipes any time you like. Nevertheless, some produce is still better and cheaper in a particular season. It's hard, for instance, to capture the full flavor of a pasta sauce made with fresh tomatoes and basil in any season but summer. And even if the ingredients involved are of good quality year-round, some dishes just taste better in a certain season, such as pasta with a hearty meat sauce in winter and pasta salad in the warm summer months. Here are our suggestions for those times when you want to cook in tune with the season.

Spring

- Penne with Roasted Asparagus and Balsamic Butter, *page 19*
- Fettuccine Alfredo with Asparagus, *page 21*
- Pasta Shells with Portobello Mushrooms, Asparagus, and Boursin Sauce, *page 23*
- Penne with Turkey, Arugula, and Sun-Dried Tomato Vinaigrette, *page 113*
- Penne Salad with Roast Beef, Arugula, Radicchio, and Capers, *page 163*
- Fettuccine with Veal, Peas, and Mint, *page 169*

Fall

- Orecchiette with Broccoli, Roasted Garlic, and Pine Nuts, *page 27*
- Fettuccine with Swiss Chard and Dried Fruit, *page 41*
- Pasta Shells with Chicken and Brussels Sprouts, *page 105*
- Spaghetti with Smoked Turkey and Leeks, *page 117*
- Bow Ties with Sweet Potatoes and Canadian Bacon, *page 141*

Summer

- Fusilli with Summer Tomato Sauce, *page 43*
- Spaghetti with Tomatoes, Black Olives, Garlic, and Feta Cheese, *page 45*
- Shells with Gazpacho Sauce and Avocado, *page 49*
- Marinated Zucchini with Bow Ties, *page 53*
- Penne Tricolore, *page 59*
- Rotelle and Shrimp with Yogurt Dill Dressing, *page 79*
- Linguine, Crab, and Avocado with Scallion Vinaigrette, *page 81*
- Bow-Tie Salad with Scallops, Black Olives, Orange, and Mint, *page 85*
- Macaroni with Summer Squash, Salami, and Ricotta Tomato Sauce, *page 133*
- Spaghetti with Creamy Corn and Ham, *page 139*

Winter

- Linguine with Cauliflower, Pine Nuts, and Currants, *page 29*
- Orecchiette with Indian-Spiced Cauliflower and Peas, *page 31*
- Ziti with Pork and Escarole in Creamy Thyme Sauce, *page 125*
- Perciatelli with Meat Sauce and Fontina, *page 155*
- Pasta Bolognese, *page 157*
- Rigatoni with Sirloin and Gorgonzola Sauce, *page 167*

LEFTOVERS

Think of leftovers as a head start; they're the original timesavers. Listed here are the recipes in this book that use cooked poultry, meat, or fish, for which precooked ingredients would be fine. You might even plan to roast a little extra chicken or beef with Sunday's dinner to save yourself a step later in the week. We also list recipes to which you could add leftovers to make a slightly different dish that is at least as good as the original.

Fish

Substitute leftover shellfish or finfish in:
- Penne with Shrimp and Spicy Tomato Sauce, *page 75*
- Shrimp Fra Diavolo with Vermicelli, *page 77*
- Rotelle and Shrimp with Yogurt Dill Dressing, *page 79*
- Linguine, Crab, and Avocado with Scallion Vinaigrette, *page 81*
- Bow-Tie Salad with Scallops, Black Olives, Oranges, and Mint, *page 85*
- Linguine Piccole with Grilled Swordfish and Parsley Anchovy Sauce, *page 87*
- Ziti with Honey Mustard Salmon, *page 89*
- Spaghetti with Tuna and Fresh Tomato Sauce, *page 93*
- Fedelini with Tuna and Chickpeas, *page 95*

Add leftover shellfish or finfish to:
- Fusilli with Summer Tomato Sauce, *page 43*
- Spaghetti with Tomatoes, Black Olives, Garlic, and Feta Cheese, *page 45*
- Penne with Salsa Verde, Mozzarella, and Cherry Tomatoes, *page 51*
- Marinated Zucchini with Bow Ties, *page 53*
- Grilled-Vegetable Pasta with Cumin, *page 57*
- Spaghetti with Parsley Almond Pesto, *page 69*
- Linguine with Gremolada, *page 71*

Poultry

Substitute leftover cooked chicken or turkey in:
- Bow Ties with Chicken, Watercress, and Walnuts, *page 97*
- Grilled-Chicken Pasta Salad with Artichoke Hearts, *page 99*
- Fettuccine with Chicken, Spinach, and Creamy Orange Sauce, *page 101*
- Pasta Shells with Chicken and Brussels Sprouts, *page 105*
- Penne with Chicken, Green Beans, and Cashew Butter, *page 111*
- Penne with Turkey, Arugula, and Sun-Dried Tomato Vinaigrette, *page 113*
- Egg Noodles with Turkey, Bacon, and Rosemary, *page 115*

Add leftover chicken or turkey to:
- Penne with Roasted Asparagus and Balsamic Butter, *page 19*
- Fettuccine Alfredo with Asparagus, *page 21*
- Pasta Shells with Portobello Mushrooms, Asparagus, and Boursin Sauce, *page 23*
- Fusilli with Artichoke Hearts and Parmesan Cream, *page 25*
- Orecchiette with Broccoli, Roasted Garlic, and Pine Nuts, *page 27*
- Spaghettini with Mushrooms, Garlic, and Oil, *page 33*
- Penne with Roasted Marsala Mushrooms, *page 35*
- Ziti with Roasted Vegetables, *page 55*
- Grilled-Vegetable Pasta with Cumin, *page 57*

Pork

Substitute leftover pork roast or chops in:
- Pasta, Tofu, Pork, and Chinese Cabbage in Ginger Broth, *page 123*
- Ziti with Pork and Escarole in Creamy Thyme Sauce, *page 125*

Add salami or pepperoni to:
- Spaghettini with Mushrooms, Garlic, and Oil, *page 33*
- Fusilli with Summer Tomato Sauce, *page 43*
- Spaghetti with Tomatoes, Black Olives, Garlic, and Feta Cheese, *page 45*
- Bow Ties with Sun-Dried Tomato and Scallion Cream, *page 47*
- Penne with Salsa Verde, Mozzarella, and Cherry Tomatoes, *page 51*
- Marinated Zucchini with Bow Ties, *page 53*

Beef

Substitute leftover roast beef or steak in:
- Penne Salad with Roast Beef, Arugula, Radicchio, and Capers, *page 163*
- Rigatoni with Sirloin and Gorgonzola Sauce, *page 167*

Add leftover roast beef or steak to:
- Orecchiette with Broccoli, Roasted Garlic, and Pine Nuts, *page 27*
- Penne with Roasted Marsala Mushrooms, *page 35*
- Ziti with Portobello Mushrooms, Caramelized Onions, and Goat Cheese, *page 37*
- Penne with Salsa Verde, Mozzarella, and Cherry Tomatoes, *page 51*
- Ziti with Roquefort Sauce, *page 63*

VEGETARIAN PASTAS

Strict vegetarians can rest assured that the recipes listed here contain no chicken stock, anchovy paste, or other hidden forbidden ingredient.

ENJOYING WINE

by Richard Marmet

Like much in life, enjoying wine is a matter of context and attitude. The wines recommended in this book are meant to be pleasurable with everyday dishes. They are wines to enjoy in the same way that you do a well-prepared, but not elaborate, meal. They should make good, simple dinners even better. To help you in buying and savoring the wines suggested in this book, keep in mind the following:

1. ***Serve what you like.*** Forget about all the complicated facts and mystique surrounding the subject. Wine's first job is to provide enjoyment, and ultimately all you need to worry about is whether you like it or not—thumbs-up or thumbs-down. Although this book provides many ideas for off-the-beaten-path wine and food combinations, if you never want to go beyond the bounds of chardonnay and cabernet sauvignon, that's fine.

2. ***Remember the effect of food.*** Sometimes a wine will be too sweet or too tannic to drink by itself. But pair it with the right dish, and all of its seeming flaws become its best attributes. Don't necessarily pass up a wine that you don't care for on its own. For example, many dishes with spicy, Asian elements go best with wines that Americans generally shy away from, such as the at times painfully acidic wines made from the chenin blanc grape.

3. ***Explore.*** One of the most exciting things about wine is its many flavors and textures. If you want to broaden your range and you know you like chardonnay, try a pinot blanc from Alsace in France, which has many of the same qualities as chardonnay. If you like merlot from California, try one from France, Italy, Long Island, Chile, or another less well-known region.

4. ***Keep unused wine.*** Don't let the fact that you can't finish a bottle of wine in one evening keep you from pulling the cork. Try putting a stopper in an unfinished bottle and keeping it for a day or two. Some young wines will actually improve in taste. And wines with even a small amount of sweetness, such as German rieslings, can often last several days without any noticeable change.

5. ***Finally, relax.*** The wine world sometimes seems peopled by a particularly snooty breed of individual with countless rules about just how and when you're supposed to enjoy wine. Forget it; it's only wine. Drink it from a juice cup. Try chilling it to see if you prefer it that way; some fruity reds such as Beaujolais or Italian dolcettos might even taste better. Mix it with seltzer if you don't want to drink too much. It's *your* wine!

Richard Marmet is one of the founders of Best Cellars, a retail shop in New York City specializing in wines for every day.

INDEX

Page numbers in **boldface** indicate photographs ❦ indicates wine recommendations

THANKS TO:

Simon Pearce Glass 120 Wooster St., New York, NY 10012: Bowl, page 36; bread basket, page 148; glasses, page 48; plates, page 30.

Wolfman-Gold & Good Company 117 Mercer St., New York, NY 10012: Bowls, pages 50, 102, 108, 112, 136, 140, 146, and 158; brass tray, page 48; bread basket, page 38; glasses, pages 56, 62, 70, 100, 110, 130, and 148; napkins, pages 54, 80, 84, 98, and 162; plates, pages 114 and 138; salt and pepper shakers, page 116; tossers, page 68.